£12.99

A GUIDE TO THE
FRESHWATER FISH
of Britain, Ireland and Europe

3 3012 00018 5753

To the Fishery Workers
without whom there would
be hardly anything to catch

A GUIDE TO THE
FRESHWATER FISH
of Britain, Ireland and Europe

Roger Phillips and Martyn Rix

Assisted by Jacqui Hurst
Layout by Jill Bryan

A Pan Original

Acknowledgements

We are particularly grateful to Tim Coles for checking the text, to Ron Greer for checking the *Salmonidae*, and to John Sutton whose help throughout the preparation of the book was invaluable.

We should also like to thank the following who contributed in many different ways: John Adams, M. Alloua, Alex Ames, Mike Andrews, Miram Aprahamian, Heikka Auvinen, Beverley Behrens, Jean Bellamy, Stan Bocking, Caroline Boisset, Dalyn Bowen, Alan Butterworth, Jean-Paul Chevalier, Tony Clarke, Jerry Domaniewski, Pamela Egremont, Nicky Foy, David Gilchrist, Andy Hart, Lauri Helin, J. Houghton, Tinge Horsfall, Jacqui Hurst, Michael Leney, J. D. Lewis, Mick Lunn, Volker Manhert, Colin Martin, Rab McMath, Nigel Mott, John Murray, Pirjo Niimnen, Ken O'Hara, David Owen, Jean-Ives Patingre, Bobby Phillips, Bob Preston, Fred Prickett, Alison Rix, John Rix, Ted Rix, Kari Selmgren, Martin Stark, Andy Thomas, Gillie Walsh-Kemmis, Stan Williams, Jacques Vedrenne, Mikko Virkajärvi, Geoffrey White, Mike Wirdnam, Nicholas de Zoete.

We were also greatly assisted by the Southern Water Authority, the North-West Water Authority, the Anglian Water Authority, Association de Pêche et de Pisciculture de l'Ardêche; Finnish Game and Fisheries Research Institute; Freshwater Fisheries Laboratory, Faskally; University of Liverpool Freshwater Fisheries Unit, University of Glasgow Department of Zoology, Freshwater Biological Association, Central Electricity Generating Board, Bristol Channel Fisheries Ltd Elver Station, Trent Fish Culture Co. Ltd, Finnish Tourist Board.

Records of British fish reproduced by kind permission of the British record (rod-caught) fish committee of the National Anglers Council, 11 Cowgate, Peterborough.

We would also like to thank Clarissa Bruce for the microscopic photograph of the scale on page 6.

ESSEX COUNTY LIB

First published in Great Britain in 1985 by
Pan Books Ltd,
Cavage Place, London SW10 9PG

9 8 7 6 5 4

Text © Roger Phillips and Martyn Rix 1985
Illustrations © Roger Phillips and Martyn Rix 1985

This book is sold subject to the condition that it
shall not, by way of trade or otherwise, be lent, re-sold,
hired out or otherwise circulated without the publisher's prior
consent in any form of binding or cover other than that in which
it is published and without a similar condition including this
condition being imposed on the subsequent purchaser.

ISBN 0 330 286900

Printed in Singapore

FE80921

Contents

Introduction 6
Acid rain 10
Fish by family 12
Glossary 13
Main text and illustrations 14
Bibliography 142
Index 143

Illustrated on the front cover:
grayling, brook lamprey, perch, burbot, blue bream.
On the back cover: flounder.
On page 1: pumpkinseed.
On title page: pike swallowing a roach.
Opposite: spined loach.
Above: nase.

Introduction

Our aim in the book has been to photograph every fish found in fresh and brackish water in Northern Europe.

The photographs of individual fish show a typical fresh specimen of average size. We have avoided outsize fish which are often ugly or damaged, and have not used immature specimens in which the proportions of head and fins to body are different. Wherever possible, we have photographed the fish while it is still alive, and as soon as it is taken from its native habitat, so that the colours are at their best. Most of the specimens were returned to the water alive.

Each species is accompanied by a photograph of its typical habitat, for example a rocky stream, an upland lake or a rich pond or estuary. Many species are very particular in their choice of habitat, others are more tolerant and can be found in many different habitats, but most have a distinct preference.

The order

The fish in this book are grouped by habitat, beginning with those which are upland or arctic in their distribution and ending with those that are primarily lowland and southern, or confined to brackish water. This should help identification as fish which are likely to be living together in the same water will appear alongside one another in the book. On page 12 the fish are listed by family according to the classification proposed by Maitland (1972) with the non-British species added.

The text

After the common English name or names the Latin name and the important European names are given to help people travelling in Europe. The Latin scientific names are very stable and most fish are still called by the names given them by Linnaeus in 1758. At the same time there are wide regional variations in fish names in living languages and these names may also change with time and fashion.

Under the heading 'Recognition and related species', the text draws attention to which details should be examined closely so that related species may be distinguished. Related species from other parts of Europe and the world are mentioned here. Useful characters are also given at the end of the text for each species, under the heading 'Characteristics'. These give details such as the number of rays in the main fins and the number of scales along the lateral line, which are not easily seen in the photographs (and often not easily seen on a living fish!).

Pharyngeal teeth are important for the identification of members of the carp family (*Cyprinidae*), especially if the fish is suspected of being a hybrid. Unfortunately, it is necessary to kill the fish to examine its pharyngeal teeth, but once the fish is dead they are easy to find. Cut off the head behind the gills and

Pharyngeal teeth of an Orfe, showing rows of 5 large and 3 smaller teeth

boil it until it begins to fall to pieces. With tweezers, or a knife and fork, lift off the gill cover (operculum), take out the gills and bone beneath them and the pharyngeal tooth will be found underneath, recognizable by its characteristic shape. The numbers of teeth and their arrangement in rows are the important characters to examine. In small specimens the teeth are very delicate and care must be taken that some of the teeth have not broken off.

Trout 'ferrox' scale enlarged 12 times

Scale reading is another important way of learning more about the individual fish. While a fish is growing the scales increase in size and each short period of growth is shown by a ring on the scale. During winter, or when growth is slow, the rings are closer together, and during periods of great stress, such as spawning, the edges of the scales, and thus the outer rings, may

Powan from Loch Lomond, photographed 24 October (see p. 43)

become eroded. By examination of a scale, therefore, at even quite small magnification (e.g. × 30), the age of a fish and the number of times it has spawned may be determined.

Recently fishery biologists have developed a technique for comparing different species or races of fish by examining their blood proteins by electrophoresis. The main uses of this have been in the taxonomy of the *Salmonidae* and the *Coregonidae* and some of the exciting possibilities arising from it are mentioned below under the species concerned, notably the brown trout (p.26).

Habitat and distribution

Under 'Habitat and distribution' the habitat preferences of each species are given briefly. This may help the fisherman decide whether a particular lake or river is likely to hold a particular species.

The natural distribution of fish in Europe has been much modified by man; the range of many species has been extended both by directly moving live fish from one area to another, and indirectly by the building of canals between waters once separated; other species have become much rarer because of pollution, the building of dams, or by increased acidification which is discussed below (p.9). In general the tolerant species (mainly *Cyprinidae*) have become commoner and more widespread, and the delicate species have become rarer (mainly *Salmonidae* and *Coregonidae*).

The original natural distribution has existed in Europe only in the last 10,000 years or so, since the last ice age. Some fish, e.g. charr or whitefish, tolerate sea water at low temperatures and were the first to migrate back into freshwater as the ice retreated. Now they are found only in cold freshwater lakes in temperate Europe, though they are still migratory in the Arctic Ocean and northern Baltic. In Lake Vanern in southern Sweden landlocked populations of salmon and smelts are found, two species which are migratory over the rest of Europe.

Some species can tolerate brackish water in northern Europe, e.g. the northern and eastern Baltic, and would have been able to enter the British Isles from a brackish North Sea. Pike, perch and roach, for example, are all common in the Baltic today. Other species will have survived further south in Europe, and migrated northwards as the climate became warmer. For instance, the barbel reached south-east England, but not the Severn system, nor Ireland which was cut off from Britain while England was still connected to the continent; the barbel has recently been introduced to the Severn and has done very well there.

Some fish, e.g. the weather loach (*Misgurnus fossilis*) failed to reach the British Isles before the Channel was formed, but today are found in northern France, Belgium and Holland. Others were brought into northern Europe by man from the south. The common carp is probably native in Europe only in the southern Danube basin, and is at the northern limit of its possible distribution in the British Isles where it can breed successfully only in warm summers.

No one today complains about the presence of carp in English waters, although they were introduced from southern Europe, probably in the fifteenth century, and kept in monastic fish ponds. Other introduced fish provoke distinctly mixed feelings among fishermen and naturalists. The rainbow trout, a native of California, is now very common all over Europe, but in Britain at least it seldom breeds naturally, and were it not for the millions raised annually in fish farms, it would be rare; as it is, it is usually stocked in place of the native brown trout.

Some foreign fish are becoming naturalized and the zander or pikeperch, a native of eastern Europe, is an example. It is now common in the rivers and canals of East Anglia and is still spreading. Recently (October 1984) one was caught in the Thames at Teddington. It is predatory on small specimens of other species, notably ruffe, perch and *Cyprinids* such as roach and bream. Because it can reduce numbers of these other species for a time, it is unpopular with many match fishermen who are happy to catch large numbers of small fish. Similar suspicions of voracity may fall upon the wels, the huge catfish also native to eastern Europe. However, one very fine fishery, at Claydon Lakes in Oxfordshire, combines an ample stock of both wels and zander as well as carp, bream, gudgeon and doubtless other native species, and in lakes in southern Finland zander live in company with numerous other species such as orfe, roach, bleak, bream, blue bream, burbot, ruffe and perch, as well as pike and trout. Attempts to introduce some other sporting species into England have been unsuccessful. Fry of Danubian salmon (p.18) were put into the Thames, but failed to become established.

Another introduced species which is likely to become commoner is the grass carp (p.104), a native of the Amur river on the borders of China and Russia. It is purely vegetarian and grows quickly, reaching, in warm climates, a weight of over 31.75 kg (70 lb). It is a very good fish for controlling water weeds in ponds and lakes, but because it requires fast water to breed, it is unlikely to become naturalized.

Breeding and growth

The next paragraph describes spawning habits and seasons. Arctic and alpine fish are adapted to short, cool summers. They spawn in autumn or winter, laying large eggs which develop slowly and hatch early in spring to give the fry the longest possible growing season. Fish from warmer climates, e.g. carp, have smaller eggs which hatch quickly; the minute fry can expect a longer growing season. Growth rates vary greatly with the amount of feed available to the individual fish, but some average figures are given to indicate the probable age of a particular fish. Most are based on measurements made in eastern England.

The likely diet of a species is indicated, in the hope that it may help the fisherman choose a suitable bait, or indicate a suitable alternative if traditional baits prove unsuccessful. Also, it can indicate which species can live together without competing for food, either by eating different items, or by exploiting a different area of water.

Fishing and cooking

The final paragraphs give some ideas on the methods which may be used for catching the fish, either by angling or some other method, and whether the fish, once caught, are likely to be edible or are best returned as soon as possible to the water. With the long coastline of the British Isles never more than a day's journey away, the British have never bothered about eating freshwater fish. Many species are popular in central Europe where fresh sea fish is unobtainable, and are unjustly neglected here. We have tried some and indicated how good they can be.

When we started we imagined that we could catch, by rod and line, most of the species for the book, but we soon found that we lacked the knowledge, skill and, above all, luck, and that we might have to wait days before catching a specimen of the desired species. We were helped to get most of the fish by fishery scientists from the various river boards, fishery departments of universities and other research bodies. They were, without exception, amazingly helpful, as well as dedicated and knowledgeable, and happily interrupted their work to get good specimens for us to photograph.

The fisheries departments of the English and Welsh Water Authorities conduct research into fish stocks, into spawning habits and into the growth rates of fish in various waters in their area, and aim to improve fisheries for the benefit of anglers by giving advice on management, and also by monitoring disease and pollution. They are financed partly by the issue of licences to anglers.

The Freshwater Biological Association also conducts research into fish as well as all other aspects of freshwater biology. It has two laboratories, one at Ambleside on Windermere, and the other near Wareham in Dorset on the river Frome. It has produced many interesting publications, including P. Maitland's *Key and Maps to British Freshwater Fishes* (1972). In Scotland, fisheries are controlled by district fishery boards which represent both owners of fishing and estuarine netting rights. Fisheries research is carried out in several laboratories operated by the Department of Agriculture and Fisheries, e.g. the Freshwater Fisheries Laboratory at Faskally near Pitlochry.

University departments of biology often have active fishery research groups. Notable among them are the University of Liverpool which operates a laboratory on Lake Bala, and Glasgow University which has a field station on Loch Lomond. In Ireland, fishery research is carried out by the Salmon Research Trust in Co. Mayo, and the Inland Fisheries Trust which also manages many of the large loughs. In France, each *département* has an organization which coordinates both fishing clubs and fish farming, the Federation Départemental des Associations Agrées de Péche et de Pisciculture. This issues fishing licences and employs fishery scientists to monitor fish stocks and improve the fishing throughout the *département*. In Finland, fishery research work is also carried out by the Finnish Game and Fisheries Research Institute which publishes journals including *Finnish Fisheries Research*, much of which is in English. A similar laboratory in Sweden, at the Institute of Freshwater Research at Drottningholm, also publishes many articles of general interest in English, and other European countries have similar bodies which control fishing and conduct research.

Diseased fish

It is uncommon to see large numbers of fish suffering from disease in the wild, but where large numbers of fish are kept close together, such as in fish farms and in waters that are over-stocked, diseases such as furunculosis, whirling disease, kidney diseases, infectious pancreatic necrosis and enteric red mouth may become serious. From these sources of infection the diseases may spread to wild fish living nearby.

Some diseases, however, have apparently appeared naturally and spread through wild populations throughout the British Isles and into Europe. One such was perch ulcer disease, which was prevalent around 1976. The Freshwater Biological Association Laboratory estimated that 99% of the perch in Lake Windermere were killed by the disease in that year, and most of the large perch throughout England died.

Salmon disease, or ulcerated dermal necrosis (U.D.N.) is another disease which has recently been widespread throughout the British Isles and in France. It was first noticed in southern Ireland in the vicinity of some fish farms, but that

A salmon suffering from ulcerated dermal necrosis showing secondary infection with the fungus Saprolegnia

may have been coincidental. It spread quickly, reaching the Solway in 1966, killing many thousands of salmon, as well as large trout. U.D.N. usually infects the head first, entering through abrasions in the skin, and causing the death of areas of flesh and muscle. These soon become infected with *Saprolegnia*, a common aquatic fungus which produces characteristic furry white patches on the skin, very conspicuous on dark fish lying in the water. When the fungus covers about half its body, the fish dies. U.D.N. is particularly virulent in cold water and infects spring salmon more than those which enter the rivers in summer; there is usually a second outbreak in autumn, but many of these fish survive long enough to spawn. The effects are now less marked than they were when the outbreak began, though in some rivers many of the spring fish are still killed. It is interesting that this is the second outbreak of U.D.N. this century. The first began on the Esk and the Nith in 1877, and lasted until the early 1920s. The disease then seemed to disappear naturally, as appears to be happening with the present outbreak.

The photographs

Most of the photographs of the fish and many of the habitats were taken on a Bronica 120 format with a 75 mm lens using extension tubes or close-up attachments when the fish were very tiny. All the pictures were taken in daylight. The remainder of the photographs were taken on a Nikon FM camera with a 50 mm lens.

The film used was Kodak Ektachrome 64 ASA pushed one stop to allow me to shoot one stop faster. On average the shots of fish were taken at f11 at 15/30 second, the problem being always having to shoot twitching fish on rotten dull days. The second problem was reflections from the silvery scales; this meant in fact choosing an exposure much darker than would have suited the background.

Acid rain

In the past few years acid rain has been the subject of many headlines, with stories of lakes and rivers being too acidic to support fish life, both in Scotland and in Norway and Sweden, and reports of hundreds of trees dying in the Black Forest. Because of the complexity of the chemical processes involved, little has been done to combat this pollution at its source, and both polluters and governments have used inconsistencies in its observed effects to avoid taking any firm action.

How acid rain kills fish

Acid water itself is harmful to fish, and when the water reaches a certain degree of acidity, fish are first unable to breed, and with increasing acidity, adults actually die. In the wild, fish often die before the critical degree of acidity is reached, because in acid water free aluminium is released from the rocks and soil, and even at very low concentrations

9

(c. 100 micrograms/litre), this free aluminium is toxic to fish. This means that a trout that can survive a certain degree of acidity without harm may be killed by the aluminium dissolved in the acid water.

The position is further complicated by the presence of other chemicals which can mitigate the toxicity of the aluminium. Calcium, commonly found in water which has been in contact with chalk or limestone, is the best antidote to aluminium. Humic acid also, which is found in brown peaty water, has some mitigating effects, at least until the water becomes very acid (less than pH 4.5).

Fish are damaged by very acid water because they are unable to keep sufficient salts in their blood, and the blood becomes too acidic. Free aluminium, absorbed by the gills, causes them to produce mucus and become clogged. Calcium acts as an antidote by being absorbed preferentially by the gills, rendering the aluminium harmless. Humic acids in peat trap some of the aluminium which would otherwise be absorbed by the fish.

Measurement of acidity

Acidity and its opposite, alkalinity, are measured in pH units. Neutral water is pH 7; alkaline water, commonly called hard water, such as comes out of springs in the chalk, has a pH of c.7.5 which is five times less acid than pH 7. Very alkaline natural waters may have a pH as high as 10, especially during surges of algal growth. The purest rain which falls, in areas of the world remote from industry, has a pH of 5.0–5.5, whereas acid rain may have a pH as low as 3.6.

Interaction of aluminium and calcium

Laboratory tests on brown trout fry (Brown 1983) compared the effects of different concentrations of aluminium and calcium at different pH levels. Most fish survived when aluminium was not present, though they began to die at pH 4.5. When aluminium was added (at 0.25 mg/1^{-1}) nearly all died at all the pH values tested, from 5.4–4.5, but when calcium (at 1.0 mg/1^{-1}) was added as well, nearly all survived; lower concentrations of calcium had little effect. At these critical levels of aluminium and calcium the actual pH had little effect, and surprisingly, survival seemed better at lower pH in the range tested.

Susceptibility of fish

Species of fish and different strains of the same species vary in their tolerance to low pH. Roach and minnows, among the *Cyprinidae*, are the most sensitive, and roach require a pH above 5.5 for egg hatch. Pike are the most tolerant of coarse fish. Members of the *Salmonidae* which are often found in upland acid waters are among the most tolerant. Field observations have shown that the lowest pH values that different species can tolerate are: salmon pH 4.6; rainbow trout pH 4.7 (the most sensitive); brown trout pH 3.9; brook trout pH 3.5 (the most tolerant). This means that brook trout can survive in water ten times more acid than rainbows or salmon.

Furthermore there are distinct variations between different strains of brook trout, and some of the more acid-tolerant strains are being experimentally stocked in Scotland.

Similar measurements of the tolerance of the different species to aluminium have not been made because it is almost impossible to measure the small concentrations involved in the field, and in natural water there are so many variables to be taken into account.

Sources of acidity

The water in lakes and rivers is acidified by several factors. Acid rain caused by industrial pollution is one, natural decay of vegetation is another. Grassland mildly acidifies water which percolates through it; bogland and especially sphagnum mosses are more active acidifiers and coniferous forests are the most damaging of all natural acidifying agents. Of the different conifers spruce (*Picea* species) are the worst acidifiers of surface water, and it has been found that streams whose watersheds have been planted soon loose all their salmon fry and many of their trout.

Acid rain events

Acid rain does not fall continuously, but, in Britain at least, only when rain-bearing clouds have passed slowly over industrial areas. Measurements at Edinburgh showed that acid rain episodes with pH less than 4 were associated with slow-moving fronts or anticyclones which had passed over the Midlands and northern Europe within the last 48 hours. In contrast clean rain of pH more than 5 was associated with air which had passed over the North Atlantic.

In many places, over a third of the acidity which falls in a year can fall in less than 5% of the wet days; that is, less than 5 days each year. It is these sudden showers of very acid water that are so damaging to fish.

Identification of waters at risk

The lakes most at risk from acid rain are those on granite rock with little soil or peat in the catchment area, and thus clear rather than peaty water. They would naturally have acid water with a pH of 5.5, caused by the natural effects of rain and what plant growth there was. Such lakes in northern Europe are likely to have become more acid during the past 100 years, and now have a pH around 5.0–4.5. It is at this low pH that damage to fish and other aquatic life is likely. A deluge of acid water following an acid rain event, or the melting of acid snow on to granite or gibbsite, produces a sudden increase in the free aluminium in the water, and the fish die. Even if similar aluminium-rich water were to enter an alkaline lake, the fish could survive because of the presence of the calcium. In very peaty water the humic acids would have a lesser mitigating effect. The results of acid rain are shown in the statistics that in parts of Scandinavia and North America over half the lakes with pH less than 5 were found to be fishless, compared with only one in seven lakes with a pH of more than 5. In the south-east of England, where most of the waters are alkaline, acid rain will have little effect, but in the granite areas of the north and west it could be catastrophic.

Didcot coal-burning power station at dawn. Water vapour can be seen coming from the cooling towers, smoke containing sulphur from the high chimney

Sources of acid rain

As we have already mentioned, acid rain events occur when rain-bearing clouds have passed over industrial areas. Of the two elements which are responsible for the acidity, sulphur and nitrogen, sulphur is by far the more important. In 1980 the United Kingdom emitted 2.3 megatonnes of sulphur and 0.62 megatonnes of nitrogen into the atmosphere, much of it in the form of oxides.

Sulphur pollution is produced mainly by burning coal. Two-thirds of it are deposited directly near its source, and a map of dry sulphur deposition shows the greatest concentrations around the coalfields, particularly in a line from Hull to Liverpool and south to Nottingham. It is the sulphur dioxide emitted by tall chimneys which is carried a long way and forms acid rain, and half of this is produced by the power stations operated by the Central Electricity Generating Board. Most of this acid rain is exported, mainly to southern Norway and Sweden on the prevailing westerly winds, and it is this long-distance transport, whether to Scotland or Scandinavia, which kills the fish in otherwise pure mountain lakes. The technology to clean up the power stations is well-known but expensive and removes the price advantage which coal at present has over oil for generating electricity.

Most of the nitrogen oxides are produced by oil burning and the exhausts from cars, and so are deposited nearer their sources. Once nitric acid rain is deposited, much of the nitrate is absorbed by plants, so it is less harmful than the sulphate which remains to acidify the soil. It is only when the nitric acid is trapped by snow or falls on bare rock that it is as harmful as the sulphuric. Although they are less important at present, emissions of nitrogen oxides are increasing while sulphur emissions are decreasing.

Other forms of pollution

Acid rain is significant as pollution mainly because it threatens lakes which are otherwise pure, and are far from industry and centres of population. Once killed, these lakes remain sterile and do not easily recover.

Enrichment or eutropification of water is the commonest type of pollution found in populated areas. Generally the fish are not killed, but the natural balance of algal growth and other aquatic life is upset by increased nitrates and phosphate from sewage, fertilisers and detergents. In rivers the problem is usually not great where the flow is sufficient; only in very dry years will excessive weed or algal growth prove harmful to fish. In lakes the problems are greater. Dense algal blooms may appear, and organic mud be deposited on to what were formerly clean gravel or marl bottoms. Mayflies and other ephemeroptera are killed and replaced by duckflies (*Chironomids*). At the same time trout stocks tend to deteriorate, and coarse fish are encouraged. Changes of this sort have occurred in the large limestone loughs in central Ireland, such as Ennel and Sheelin, and in Loch Leven in central Scotland. Some of the more delicate species may become extinct, as occurred in Loch Maben, where the lake which formerly held vendace is now a productive bream fishery. Lowland reservoirs in England are often eutrophic. but support trout because of regular stocking and the removal of coarse fish.

Acute pollution

Acid rain and eutropification may be thought of as insidious pollution, as their effects are largely cumulative, even though fish may die in large numbers at one time. Acute pollution kills fish often more effectively, but its effects are short-lived and the river or lake may recover in a year or so. The damage is usually due to carelessness, with chemicals, often pesticides or weedkillers, or with overflow of sewage or silage, the latter being especially toxic. Fish may also be killed by suspended effluent from paper mills, and where these are sited near the sea, the effects on salmon smolts migrating in low water conditions may be disastrous.

If any numbers of fish are found dead or dying, they should be reported, as soon as possible, to the local water authority, either by dialling the emergency number given under the local water authority, or by dialling 999.

Index of fish by family

Sturgeon family *Acipenseridae*
Sturgeon *Acipenser sturio* Linn. p.124

Herring family *Clupeidae*
Allis shad *Alosa alosa* Linn. p.126
Twaite shad *Alosa fallax* Lacépède p.126

Salmon family *Salmonidae*
Salmon *Salmo salar* Linn. pp.18–23
Sea trout *Salmo trutta trutta* Linn. pp.32–5
Brown trout *Salmo trutta fario* Linn. pp.26–31
Rainbow trout *Salmo gairdneri* Richardson pp.36–9
Charr *Salvelinus alpinus* Linn. pp.14–17
Brook trout *Salvelinus fontinalis* Mich. p.24

Whitefish family *Coregonidae*
Houting *Coregonus lavaretus* Linn. p.41
Powan *Coregonus wartmanni* Bloch p.43
Schelly *Coregonus nilssoni* Valenciennes p.40
Vendace *Coregonus vandesius* Richardson p.42
Sikloja *Coregonus albula* Linn. p.42
Pollan *Coregonus autumnalis pollan* Thompson p.43

Grayling family *Thymallidae*
Grayling *Thymallus thymallus* Linn. p.44

Smelt family *Osmeridae*
Smelt *Osmerus eperlanus* Linn. p.130

Pike family *Esocidae*
Pike *Esox lucius* Linn. pp.70–3

Carp family *Cyprinidae*
Carp *Cyprinus carpio* Linn. pp.96–101
Crucian carp *Carassius carassius* Linn. p.102
Goldfish *Carassius auratus* Linn. p.100
Bitterling *Rhodeus sericeus* Bloch p.110
Tench *Tinca tinca* Linn. p.106
Barbel *Barbus barbus* Linn. p.64
Mediterranean barbel *Barbus meridionalis* Risso p.62
Gudgeon *Gobio gobio* Linn. p.94
Silver bream *Blicca bjoerkna* Linn. p.90
Common bream *Abramis brama* Linn. p.88
Blue bream *Abramis ballerus* Linn. p.92
Vimba *Vimba vimba* Linn. p.124
Chekhon *Pelecus cultratus* Linn. p.124
Schneider *Alburnoides bipunctatus* Bloch p.57
Bleak *Alburnus alburnus* Linn. p.78
Asp *Aspius aspius* Linn. p.80
Nase *Chondrostoma nasus* Linn. p.66
Toxostome *Chondrostoma toxostoma* Vallot p.58
Belica *Leucaspius delineatus* Heckel p.79
Minnow *Phoxinus phoxinus* Linn. p.46
Blageon *Leuciscus souffia* Risso p.56
Dace *Leuciscus leuciscus* Linn. p.60
Orfe *Leuciscus idus* Linn. p.84
Chub *Leuciscus cephalus* Linn. p.68
Roach *Rutilus rutilus* Linn. p.82
Grass carp *Ctenopharyngodon idella* Valenciennes p.104
Rudd *Scardinius erythrophthalmus* Linn. p.86

Loach family *Cobitidae*
Spined loach *Cobitis taenia* Linn. p.120
Stone loach *Noemacheilus barbatulus* Linn. p.48

Catfish family *Siluridae*
Wels *Silurus glanis* Linn. p.108

American catfish family *Ictaluridae*
American catfish *Ictalurus melas* Rafin. p.110

Eel family *Anguillidae*
Eel *Anguilla anguilla* Linn. p.122

Cod family *Gadidae*
Burbot *Lota lota* Linn. p.118
Pouting *Trisopterus luscus* Linn. p.136

Stickleback family *Gasterosteidae*
Three-spined stickleback *Gasterosteus aculeatus* Linn. p.116
Ten-spined stickleback *Pugnitius pugnitius* Linn. p.117

Pipefish family *Syngnathidae*
Greater pipefish *Syngnathus acus* p.128
Deep-snouted pipefish *Syngnathus typhle* p.128
Nilsson's pipefish *Syngnathus rostellatus* p.128
Straight-nosed pipefish *Nerophis ophidion* p.128

Mullet family *Mugilidae*
Thin-lipped grey mullet *Mugil ramada* Risso p.138
Thick-lipped grey mullet *Mugil labrosus* Risso p.138
Golden grey mullet *Mugil auratus* Risso p.138

Sea bass family *Serranidae*
Sea bass *Dicentrarchus labrax* Linn. p.140

Perch family *Percidae*
Perch *Perca fluviatilis* Linn. p.74
Zander *Stizostedion lucioperca* Linn. p.76
Ruffe *Gymnocephalus cernua* Linn. p.78
Apron *Zingel asper* Linn. p.54

Sunfish family *Centrarchidae*
Largemouth bass *Micropterus salmoides* Lacépède p.114
Pumpkinseed *Lepomis gibbosus* Linn. p.112

Goby family *Gobidae*
Common goby *Pomatoschistus microps* Kroyer p.136

Gurnard family *Triglidae*
Tub gurnard *Trigla lucerna* Linn. p.128
Red gurnard *Aspertrigla cuculus* Day p.129

Bullhead family *Cottidae*
Bullhead *Cottus gobio* Linn. p.50
Siberian bullhead *Cottus poecilopus* Heckel p.50

Flatfish family *Pleuronectidae*
Flounder *Platichthys flesus* Linn. p.132
Plaice *Pleuronectes platessa* Linn. p.134
Dab *Limanda limanda* Linn. p.134

Sole family *Soleidae*
Sole *Solea solea* Linn. p.134

Turbot family *Scophthalmidae*
Brill *Scophthalmus rhombus* Linn. p.134

Lamprey family *Petromyzonidae*
Sea lamprey *Petromyzon marinus* Linn. p.52
Lampern *Lampetra fluviatilis* Linn. p.52
Brook lamprey *Lampetra planeri* Bloch p.52

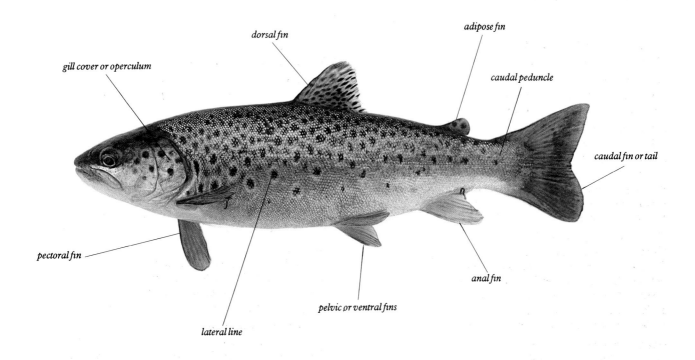

gill cover or operculum

dorsal fin

adipose fin

caudal peduncle

caudal fin or tail

pectoral fin

anal fin

pelvic or ventral fins

lateral line

Glossary

adipose (fin)   Small fleshy fin between dorsal fin and tail, characteristic of salmon and related families (see above).

anadromous   Fish, such as salmon, which spawn in freshwater, but feed primarily in the sea (c.f. *catadromous*).

anal (fin)   Fin between anus and tail (see above).

barbel   Small fleshy appendages on outside of mouth of carp, barbel and related fish, used for tasting.

brackish   Water between sea and fresh, of low salinity.

catadromous   Fish, such as eels, which feed in freshwater, but spawn in the sea.

caudal (fin)   The 'tail' fin (see above).

caudal peduncle   Narrow part of a fish body between fins and 'tail' (see above).

cyprinids   Carp family, usually used for roach, bream, bleak etc.

dapping   Fishing with a very long rod, a light line which is carried out by the wind, and a large bushy dry fly or natural insect.

dorsal (fin)   The fin on the back of the fish (see above).

electrophoresis   The visual separation and comparison of proteins, by running them through an electrically charged film of gel; the different proteins move at different speeds.

enzyme   Biological compounds, usually complex proteins, which enable physiological reactions to occur; they may be useful genetic markers.

finnock   Young sea trout, from Gaelic *fin* meaning white, used in Scottish highlands, c.f. whitling.

fry   Young fish, less than one year old.

gill cover   Two hard semi-circular flaps on either side of the head of a fish, covering the gills (see above).

gonad   The reproductive organs of an animal.

kyp   A hook on the end of the lower jaw, esp. of salmon, which forms in males at spawning.

lateral line   A line of perforated scales along the side of a fish.

milt   Milk-like sperm of fish.

parr   Small young salmon, 1–3 years old, before going to sea, and trout of similar size.

pectoral (fin)   Pair of fins nearest to gills (see above).

pelagic   Fish which live near the surface, usually of the sea.

pelvic (fin)   Pair of fins on the belly of the fish (see above).

pharyngeal teeth   Pair of teeth at the base of the mouth, useful for the identification of *Cyprinidae* (see p.6).

prides   Young of lampreys, living in fresh water.

rakers (gill)   Rake or comb-like bones between the mouth and gills of fish, which filter food from the water and prevent it being lost through the gill openings.

redd   Nest of stones made by fish, usually a hollow in a gravel bed on the bottom of the river.

scale   Small transparent circular plate, embedded in the skin of most fish (see p.6).

smolt   Young salmon or sea trout on first migration from river to sea.

spate   Sudden flood in a river caused by heavy rain or melting snow.

tubercle   Small knob or swelling.

ventral (fin)   Pair of fins on belly of fish, an alternative name for the pelvic fins.

vomer   Bone in the centre of the roof of the mouth of fish, sometimes bearing teeth.

whitling   Young sea trout on its first return from the sea to the river, used esp. on river Tweed.

Charr. Female from Crummock Water, Cumberland. Photographed 27 August with plants of quillwort washed up by a storm.

Charr, male form from Loch Lee, Angus. Photographed 11 June.

Loch Lee, Angus.

Charr

Charr, Arctic charr, *Salvelinus alpinus* Linn. Family *Salmonidae*.
French, omble-chevalier; German, See-saibling, Wandersaibling
(Swiss); Dutch, beekridder; Swedish, roding; Finnish, nieria.

Recognition and related species

In shape the charr is very similar to the trout, but its back is usually
greenish or bluish with numerous pale spots, and the belly, in the male at
least, has some trace of yellow, orange or pink. In the spawning season
this colour is especially bright, and the leading edges of the fins are then
pure white. The females are usually duller coloured, primarily greenish
or bluish with little or no red on the underparts.

Though very variable, all European charrs are thought to belong to the
same species, but there are other species in North America. The
commonest of these is the brook trout (*S. fontinalis*) described on p.24.
It differs in having a heavily marked back, the pattern running into the
dorsal fin and tail.

The Dolly Varden (*S. malma*) from the northwest of North America,
eastern Siberia and Korea, has recently been shown to be very closely
related to the Arctic charr, or even merely a predatory form of it rather
than a distinct species. Both anadromous (sea-going) and land-locked
races are known, and specimens up to 14.5 kg (32 lb) are recorded. It
has a dark greenish body with pale spots or silvery with a bluish back in
sea-run specimens.

Habitat and distribution

Charr are found in rivers in the Arctic, south to Iceland and central
Norway, around 64°N. These populations are anadromous, spawning in
fresh water, often in short, glacier-fed streams e.g. in Greenland. In the
sea most remain quite close to their parent rivers, usually within 100 km
(62½ miles) of its mouth, but individual specimens have been known to
travel long distances and enter other rivers.

South of 64°N charr are found mainly in deep cold lakes in the
mountains, or at lower altitudes in the north and west of the British Isles.
Here each population has been land-locked and isolated for several

thousand years. The charr tend to live in shoals at great depth and may
be seen only when they spawn or come to the surface in the late evening
to feed. About 200 lochs have populations of charr today and in one or
two, e.g. Lough Neagh and Loch Leven they have become extinct in
modern times. Some of these populations have not evolved any
interesting characters, others, either by genetic drift during their long
isolation, or in response to local conditions, have become sufficiently
modified to lead some authorities to consider them separate species.
C. Tate Regan who studied British charr in detail around the beginning
of the century recognized fifteen species. Some such as *S. willughbii* are
widespread in the Lake District and Scotland, others are restricted to
one or two small highland lakes; e.g. *S. perisii* in North Wales,
S. struanensis in Loch Rannoch, *S. gracillimus* on Shetland, *S. grayi* in
Lough Melvin, *S. fimbriatus* in Lough Coomasaham in Co. Kerry,
S. scharfii in Lough Owel in Co. Westmeath. These are among the more
distinct and differ from one another in such characteristics as colour, size
and shape of head and mouth bones, number of scales along the lateral
line, and size of eye.

In addition to this type of geographical variation, more than one distinct
population of charr may co-exist in a large lake (compare with trout
pp.24–39, whitefish pp.40–3). Typically a dwarf race may be found near
the shore or on the bottom, while a larger race lives in open water. In one
lake in Norway the small, slow growing form reaches a maximum of
50 gm (2 oz) and averages 20 gm (1¾ oz), the large fast-growing form
averages 700–800 gm (1½–1¾ lb) and reaches a maximum of 3.6 kg
(8 lb). In Lake Windermere two races are found though the distinctions
between them are less obvious; they spawn at different times and in
different areas of the lake.

In Lake Geneva the charr remain at great depth, over 100 m (330 ft) in
summer when the surface water is warm. They are also found in the Lac
du Bourget and have been introduced into other lakes in the Auvergne
and in the Pyrenees.

Breeding and growth

Charr spawn in redds (hollows) in gravel or over boulder-strewn lake
beds. In the Arctic the redds are in rivers, further south either in streams

15

Lake Windermere, Lake District.

flowing into lakes or in the lakes themselves. Spawning takes place between September and March and usually at night. In Windermere the smaller fish usually spawn in shallow water or in the River Brathay around the middle of November, the larger fish spawn in deeper water in February.

Growth is very variable from population to population. Sea-run individuals have been known to reach 12 kg (27 lb) and an age of forty years. The largest form in the British Isles is probably that from Lough Owel which may reach 1.4 kg (3 lb). These land-locked charr probably live to a maximum of ten years.

Feeding

Charr mostly depend on small invertebrates for food. When two populations were living together, the bottom-living fish were found to eat mainly *Gammarus*, a freshwater shrimp, and other bottom-living invertebrates, those living in open water fed on *Daphnia* and surface insects. A sample of the stomach contents of the charr illustrated here from the Lake District contained 90% *Daphnia hyalina*, with 10% *Bythotrephes longimanus* and *Cyclops strenuus abyssorum*. A few populations are mainly fish-eating.

Fishing for charr

Sea-run charr take flies freely and are often caught on spinning tackle, mostly on small spoons.

The lake populations vary greatly in the ease with which they can be caught. Sometimes they take flies freely on the surface; even those which normally live at great depth come to the surface in shoals on warm evenings and take tiny flies.

Although they feed mainly on plankton, deep-living charr may be caught on small spoons. Traditional charr-fishing gear in the Lake District consists of a large rudder-shaped lead weight weighing about

750 gm (1½ lb) to which is attached a line with small silver and copper spoons at 3 m (10 ft) intervals. Normally six or seven spoons are used, so that the lowest is fishing 21 m (70 ft) below the surface, the uppermost 3 m (10 ft) below. Two stout rods are used in each boat; a small bell at the end of the rod registers a take from a charr. At each take the line is hauled up and the charr, if still attached, is taken into the boat. In some lakes charr take wet flies intended for trout; Haweswater and Loch Doon are both said to have free-rising charr, and those in Loch Lee on the North Esk are often caught on the fly.

The British rod-caught record is 3 lb 4 oz (1.48 kg), caught by S. C. Rex on 23 October 1982 from Loch Dubhlochan, Knoydart, Inverness-shire.

Cooking charr

Charr usually have firm, pale pink or white flesh and make excellent eating. They can be cooked in the same way as small trout. Formerly, potted charr was a speciality of Windermere; the fish were cooked and the flesh separated from the bone before being mixed with melted butter and seasoned with pepper, mace and nutmeg. They were then sealed with clarified butter and exported, for example to Fortnum and Mason in London.

Characteristics

Dorsal fin: 12–13 rays.
Anal fin: 12 rays.
Adipose fin present, unspotted.
Teeth confined to the head of the vomer.
Scales in the lateral line: 180–240.

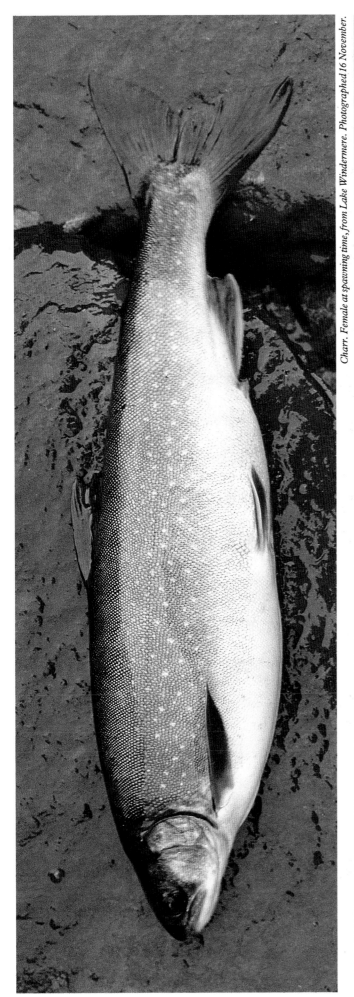

Charr. Female at spawning time, from Lake Windermere. Photographed 16 November.

Charr. Male at spawning time, from Lake Windermere. Photographed 16 November.

17

Salmon

Salmon. *Salmo sadar* Linn. Family *Salmonidae*. French, saumon;
German, Lachs; Swedish, lax; Finnish, lohi.

Recognition and related species

A mature salmon can easily be recognized by its large size, silver body
with few black spots, and by the small dark adipose fin characteristic of
the salmon family.

Large sea trout and salmon can be difficult to tell apart; salmon have
fewer spots, a more forked tail with stiffer outer rays and a narrower
'wrist' to the tail, than sea trout of the same size; salmon have 10–13
scales between the adipose fin and the lateral line and 10–12 rays in the
dorsal fin, trout have 13–16 scales and 8–10 branched dorsal fin rays.
Detailed examination of the scales may also aid the identification of
doubtful specimens. A 5 kg (11 lb) salmon is likely to have spent one or
two winters at sea, and will at most have spawned once. A sea trout of
this size will have spawned at least twice or even three times, and the
distinction will be even clearer in larger fish. The number of spawnings
can be told by examining the growth rings on the scales, so scales of any
doubtful specimens can be kept and sent to an expert for study.

Salmon and trout can now be distinguished by electrophoresis of the
enzyme proteins in their blood, and this method has enabled salmon x
trout hybrids to be identified with certainty. Studies of a large number of
salmon have indicated that an average of just under $1/2$% are hybrids with
trout, although in some rivers, notably the Coquet in Northumberland,
the proportion has been found to be higher, nearly 1%. Two races of
salmon have been recognized in the British Isles, a boreal race which was
isolated in the North Sea area, and a Celtic race which remained south of
the ice sheets in the last glaciation, and repopulated Western Europe
and the west coasts of Britain.

During their stay in the river salmon change greatly in colour, becoming
pinkish and finally brick-red in the males, dark greyish in the females,
and sea trout go through similar changes, though never becoming so red.
At the immature or parr stage, salmon and trout are also very similar;
both have small red and black spots, as well as dark vertical bars along
their backs, so-called parr marks. In salmon there are 10–12, in trout
9–10. Salmon parr also have fewer spots on their dorsal fins, and on the
operculum or gill cover. The fin ray characters found in the adults are
also present in the parr. A salmon parr also appears to have a blunter
head because the maxillary bone extends back only as far as the eye,
while it goes farther back than the eye in a trout.

The Pacific salmon belong to a different genus, *Oncorhynchus*. Two
species have been introduced into the White Sea area of Arctic Russia
and become established there, the Chum salmon, *O. keta* which is
unspotted and the humpback salmon *O. gorbuscha*. Stray humpback
salmon sometimes appear in rivers in northern Britain. They may be
distinguished from Atlantic salmon by their small size, spotted tail and
dorsal fin and by the large number of rays in the anal fin (14–16). They
are much less spotted than rainbow trout. A third species, the coho,
O.kisutch, has been introduced into Europe for fish farming, and may
escape. It has small black spots on the back and sides along the lateral
line, and on the upper lobe only of the tail.

Other interesting relatives of salmon are found in eastern Europe. The
Danubian salmon, *Hucho hucho* is becoming rare in the Danube and its
tributaries, but has been successfully introduced into the Rhine in
eastern France and the Usses in Savoie. The body is silvery or reddish
with black spots, and it can reach 120 cm (48 in) in length and 21 kg
(46 lb) in weight. The might taimen, *H. taimen* from the rivers of Siberia
such as the Ob and Lena is even bigger, up to 80 kg (176 lb). A second
genus, *Salmothymus* has two species in Europe, *S. obtusirostris* in rivers
along the Dalmatian coast, and *S. ochridanus*, a much smaller
landlocked form in the limestone Lake Ochrid on the borders of
Yugoslavia and Albania. They have blunt heads and silvery bodies with
scattered spots.

Habitat and distribution

Salmon require unpolluted and well-oxygenated water to survive, and
stony streams for the parr in their first few years of life. In addition the
adults need an unimpeded run upstream from the sea to the spawning
grounds. Hydro-electricity dams, and pollution, particularly of
estuaries, have caused it to become extinct in many of the rivers of the
Baltic and western Europe as well as in North America. The distribution
of the salmon in the sea is on both sides of the North Atlantic as far north

A salmon pool on the river Don, Aberdeenshire.

as Iceland and southern Greenland, and in the Baltic. It spawns from the
Minho river on the border of Spain and Portugal to the Kola peninsula in
Arctic Russia, and in Canada and in the United States south to the
Connecticut river. Land-locked populations are found in several lakes,
notably in southern Sweden.

Many attempts have been made to introduce salmon into the southern
hemisphere, so far without success, though land-locked populations
have been established in New Zealand.

Breeding and growth

Salmon spawn in shallow gravelly areas of rivers and streams. Males and
females tend to swim together for much of their time in the river but
pairing takes place in the pools near the spawning beds. In some rivers,
such as the Aberdeenshire Dee, the salmon can start to spawn as early as
September, but November and December are the usual months in most
rivers.

The female selects a suitable area of gravel in water about 30 cm (1 ft)
deep, with a good flow over it. She makes a depression about 15 cm
(6 in) deep by turning on her side and vigorously flapping her tail. The
male meanwhile swims beside her, driving off other fish which come too
near. When the depression is ready it usually has two or three larger
stones in the bottom and it is among these that the eggs are laid and
immediately fertilized by the quivering male. Then the male moves
away, and the female, by more flapping, sends down gravel to cover the
eggs.

It is interesting that male parr are usually found on the spawning beds.
They are sexually mature, and probably fertilize at least some of the
eggs as they tend to lie right in the bed as the female is laying. About 70%
of male parr have been found to be capable of spawning, but female parr
have never been found with ripe eggs. The eggs are orange, about 6 mm
($1/3$ in) across, and hatch after three months or so into alevins, but still
stay hidden in the gravel for a further month, by which time they are 0.5
cm ($1/4$ in) long. For the next few years the parr live in streams or in
shallow parts of rivers. In richer rivers they may migrate to the sea after
only one year, whereas in most rivers three years is normal and in very
poor waters they may migrate only after seven or eight years. At about
12.5 cm (5 in) in length the parr begin to move downstream in shoals,
and as they approach sea water they become silvery and are known as
smolts; their main movement to the sea is in April and May. After
reaching the sea the young salmon move northwards to the feeding

Salmon from river Tay, Perthshire. A fresh grilse with sea lice above the anal fin. Photographed 24 September.

Salmon from river Tay, Perthshire. A large autumn fish, darker in colour, showing that it is some time since it came up from the sea. Photographed 22 September.

Salmon parr from river Don, Aberdeenshire. Photographed 4 September.

grounds. As recently as 1956 it was not known where salmon went in the sea, but in that year a salmon was caught off west Greenland that had been tagged as a smolt in the Blackwater river in Ross-shire. A large number of salmon are now known to travel across the northern Atlantic to feeding grounds in the Davis strait off western Greenland. Both European (particularly those from France) and North American salmon feed here, and soon after this discovery an important fishery grew up. Other salmon feeding grounds are located in the Norwegian sea north of the Faroes and around the Lofoten Islands, and another sea fishery has recently grown up in these areas.

The Baltic salmon do not feed in the Atlantic, but in the southern Baltic, mainly around the islands of Bornholm and Gotland, and in international waters between Sweden and Lithuania. Here also they are plundered at sea, especially by Danish fishermen, to the severe detriment of the spawning stocks in Swedish and Finnish rivers.

The majority of salmon return to the rivers in which they spawned, and probably even to the same area of the river. There has been much conjecture about how a salmon can tell if it has arrived in the sea off its own river, but it is likely that smell is the major factor, and that it can remember the smell of its natal water. Probably less than one salmon in a thousand makes a mistake and swims up a strange river, and salmon populations from even nearby have been found to be remarkably distinct genetically. The implication of this discovery for exploitation and management of the fisheries is that each river should be considered as a distinct entity. Ideally, salmon should only be caught in the estuaries and the rivers so that the stocks in each river can be watched and exploited without danger of overfishing and leaving an insufficient number of spawning fish.

The percentage of smolts which return as mature salmon has been found to vary greatly, and at present the numbers which would return under natural conditions are greatly reduced by the fisheries off Greenland and the Faroes, by coastal drift netting off Ireland and Northumberland and by the depredations of grey and other seals which have increased dramatically after being protected by law. In one of the earliest large-scale tagging experiments in the river Tay in 1905, 1.7% of tagged smolts were later caught. This could suggest that about 5% of smolts were returning as salmon. Another experiment, in North America,

recorded a return of 3%. Recently, in Iceland, where there is no netting of salmon in the sea, 9.4% of smolts returned, but these fish were mainly small and had not travelled far but remained near the coast. Another recent survey, in Ireland, recorded a return of 2.4%.

The length of time salmon spend feeding in the sea varies greatly, and has a direct bearing on their final size. Many come back to spawn after one winter in the sea, usually in the summer of the year following that in which they entered the sea as smolts. These fish are known as grilse, and vary in size from 1.5 to 4.5 kg (3–10 lb). Most salmon return after two years in the sea, at a weight about double that of grilse, others remain in the sea up to 4½ years, and these are the ones that weigh from 18 to 27.5 kg (40–60 lb) when caught.

There is evidence that grilse mostly originate from parr which have spent three years or more in the river, and that the larger fish grow from parr which spend less time in the river. The higher growth rate of parr in fertile rivers such as the Wye and the Dorset Stour, or in the lower reaches of large rivers such as Tweed and Tay, could account for the greater numbers of large fish in these rivers compared with the more acid rivers of the north and west coasts of Scotland, which may have as numerous, but generally smaller fish. Their higher growth rate when young is continued and reflected in later maturity and return to spawn. The largest may be six or seven years old.

Most salmon die after spawning, but a significant number survive and return a second time to spawn. It is likely that most of these fish do not travel all the way to the arctic feeding grounds, but remain near the river in which they spawned. They return for their second spawning usually within a year and at double or more the weight at which they re-entered the sea. The percentage of second spawners varies considerably in different rivers, from 0.6 to 34%. Nearly all are females and can be identified by having more spots on their gill covers, and by their scales. Salmon enter fresh water at all times of year. The timing of the runs varies from river to river, and is often reflected in the different dates of the close seasons. In general fish which enter the rivers before November will spawn the same year, whereas those which arrive later will remain almost a whole year in the rivers before they spawn. On the Bundrowes river draining Lough Melvin the season opens on 1 January, and on the Tay on 15 January, but in late rivers the season may not open

Spawning stream in the western highlands of Scotland, at low water.

until April, and even then significant numbers of fish may not enter the river until the summer.

The percentages of fish which enter a river at any time may also vary greatly over a period of years. Each movement of fish is called a run; the spring run on a river may steadily decline, while the summer and autumn runs may improve. The reasons why this happens are not clear, but it is likely that the timing of the runs is partly hereditary, and partly dependent on the distance of the main feeding grounds from the coast. During periods of colder climate in the subarctic, e.g. the 1880s, the main feeding grounds were further south and the runs were mainly of grilse and summer salmon. Similarly during periods of warmer climate, e.g. 1920–50, the warmest period for thousands of years, the feeding grounds moved north again, and most salmon arrived in spring after spending longer in the sea. In recent years spring runs have declined dramatically in most rivers, and a higher percentage of salmon has been entering the rivers in summer and autumn.

Salmon tend to congregate in the estuaries, waiting for a suitable flood or spate in which they can more easily swim across shallows and up rapids. In dry periods large numbers may be seen moving up and falling back with the tide, and it is at this time that most were traditionally caught by commercial netsmen. Pollution in estuaries may also have a serious effect, especially in hot, dry summers, and large numbers of fish may die.

In suitable flood conditions the fish may move upstream very quickly, travelling by day and night. In a long river like the Loire, the salmon reach as far as 640 km (400 miles) from the sea by the beginning of March, and they have been recorded to cover 400 km (250 miles) in ten days. They do not always move with such a sense of urgency in shorter rivers, and tend to remain in pools in the lower reaches if the water is very cold.

Salmon may leap quite high falls in their run upstream, and one of these salmon leaps while the fish are running is a spectacular sight. The word salmon is derived from the Latin word for leap, and place names such as Leixlip, on the Liffey river in Ireland, refer to this and to the old Norse name for salmon, lax. The fish also leap high out of the water while they are resting in pools; sometimes this seems to be when they have been disturbed, sometimes when they are getting restless and preparing to continue upstream, sometimes when they are running, but often for no clear reason.

While in fresh water, and especially when the rivers are low, salmon tend to congregate in deeper pools. They have a preference for well oxygenated water, and in slower rivers lie below rapids or weirs. Successive generations tend to lie in exactly the same places and these 'lies' are well known to fishermen. Some are only occupied in high water, some most of the time.

Many salmon rivers, and they are among the most prolific, have lakes along their length which provide a good resting place for salmon, especially in times of drought. Here they tend to lie in about 3 m (10 ft) of water, along the shores or shallows. In times of flood they congregate where fresh water enters the lake, ready to move up to the spawning beds.

During the period they are in fresh water their body weight slowly decreases and their gonads increase in size and weight at the expense of muscle tissue. The males develop a hook on the lower jaw, the kyp, and the upper jaw also elongates and curves downwards.

Feeding

In the sea, salmon probably feed on small fish such as sand eels and capelins, on shrimps and other pelagic animals. The land-locked salmon of Lake Vanern in southern Sweden, which grow to a weight of about

The Falls of Feugh, a salmon leap in Aberdeenshire.

5 kg (11 lb) after three years in the lake, feed primarily on vendace (p.42) and smelts (p.134).

Mature salmon never feed in fresh water, in fact there is evidence that they begin their fast some time before leaving the sea. The reason they take flies, worms, boiled prawns etc in fresh water has never been properly explained, but it is probably because of a reflex action triggered by its memory of food. It is an interesting thought that if a run of large greedily feeding salmon entered a river, they would soon decimate their own parr and smolt population, which would be the major source of food available.

Fishing for salmon

More has probably been written about salmon fishing than about fishing for all other species put together. This is as much because of its unpredictability as of the value and sporting quality of the catch. Salmon do not feed in fresh water, but they may take in their mouths anything that attracts them. Salmon are commonly caught with worms, prawns, minnows, spinners and flies of almost any type, from gaudy monsters a few inches long to tiny tufts of black hair or hackle. Sometimes they will ignore everything, at other times seize a large spoon, or delicately suck down a small fly intended for a trout. In general salmon become most active when the water is high and presumably, therefore, well oxygenated. They take best as the river is rising after rain, and as it is dropping again. Fresh, rather windy weather with some cloud, is better than hot, sunny, or close thundery weather. In colder water the salmon lie nearer the bed of the river and tend to take under water, but in warmer water they will rise and take flies fished just under the surface. In general larger flies are better in cold or high water, and smaller flies when the water is low and warm. Dry fly fishing for salmon has never been very successful in Europe, though it is practised in North America. Local knowledge is invaluable when salmon fishing, as the salmon use the same lies year after year at specific heights of water, and they take more freely in some lies than in others. During floods they will rest behind large stones, often close to the bank, while in low water they will be in deeper faster places, usually in the main current. Though they are in many ways very similar, there are one or two basic differences between salmon and trout fishing. When a trout takes a fly it is necessary to strike reasonably quickly to drive the hook into the fish before it can spit out the fly. A salmon spits out the fly much more slowly, usually after it has returned to its lie with the fly in its mouth, so striking should be delayed until the fish has hooked itself. A trout will usually not come a second time after it has missed a fly or avoided it at the last minute. A salmon will often take the fly a second or third time, and be hooked on its later attempt. For some the unpredictability of salmon fishing is part of its attraction, and there is no doubt that ample perseverence and patience are needed. Others prefer the greater knowledge and skill needed for catching large wild trout.

The record British rod-caught salmon is still that of 28 kg (64 lb) caught by Miss G. W. Ballantine on the Tay in October 1922. Bigger ones have been caught in Norway such as the one of 34 kg (75 lb) hooked on a fly and landed after a twelve-hour fight. Even bigger ones have been caught in the nets including one of 38 kg (84 lb).

Cooking salmon

Salmon are excellent to eat, particularly cold smoked, and have always been prized as food fish. Sadly, there is apparently no substance in the oft-repeated story that the indentures of apprentices, in London or elsewhere, stipulated that they should not be fed salmon more than three days a week. Even in 1800 when salmon were still caught in the Thames, they sold at an average of ten shillings a pound, and a 20 lb fish caught at Surley Hall just above Windsor, was sold to the King for a guinea a pound. From about 1830 to 1976 the Thames was too polluted for any salmon to survive the journey up its estuary to fresh water, but attempts since 1977 to re-establish the run by planting parr in the headwaters seem to have a chance of succeeding, as several adult salmon were seen in the Thames system in 1983.

The growing of salmon in cages in the sea, particularly in the fjords of western Norway and the sea lochs of Scotland, has grown immensely in recent years, and has overtaken in value the commercial catch of wild salmon. In spring 1984, for the first time, the price of wild fish has been kept down by the amount of farmed salmon on the market.

Hopefully this will relieve some of the pressure on the wild fish.

Characteristics

Dorsal fin: 10–12 rays.
Anal fin: 11 rays.
Adipose fin present.
Scales between adipose fin and lateral line: 10–13.

Female salmon in breeding colours, river Lune. Photographed 17 November.

Male salmon in breeding colours, river Lune. Note large kyp on lower jaw. Photographed 17 November.

23

Little Thompson river, Colorado, U.S.A.

American brook trout

American brook trout, speckled trout, speckled charr. *Salvelinus fontinalis* Mitchill. Family *Salmonidae*. French, saumon de fontaine; German, Bachsaibling; Dutch, bronforel; Finnish, puronieria.

Recognition and related species

The American brook trout is strictly speaking a charr rather than a trout, but it is trout-like in shape and habits. In colour it is very distinctive, having a beautifully marbled back, the marbling extending over the dorsal fin and the tail, and there is a black stripe on the anal fin. Like the European native charr, the male becomes red underneath in the spawning season, and the leading edges of the fins are white. Its tail is nearly square.

A second American charr is the so-called lake trout, *S. namaycash* found in deep cold lakes. It reaches 45 kg (102 lb) in weight and is covered all over with bean-shaped light spots on a greenish ground; its tail is deeply forked. It has been introduced into Sweden, Denmark and some of the large Alpine and Pyrenean lakes.

Habitat and distribution

In North America the brook trout is found as a native species in streams in the Atlantic provinces of Canada southward to Cape Cod, and in the Appalachians south to Georgia, as well as across the Great Lakes to Minnesota and north to Hudson Bay. It has since been introduced to Europe, New Zealand, Asia and South America. Both anadromous and wholly freshwater populations are known; sea-run specimens are silvery to purplish with red spots on the sides.

In England the brook trout has not been very successful, though introduced as early as 1869. Small populations have established themselves in Sussex, in one or two places in the west of England and in central Scotland. In France brook trout have been introduced into several streams, notably in the Auvergne, the Savoie and the Pyrenees.

Breeding and growth

Spawning takes place in winter, in October and November in much the same way as trout, in both running and standing water. Young fry have parr markings. Growth is variable; the average adult length is 25–30 cm (10–12 in). Maximum size is about 6.5 kg (14¼ lb).

Feeding

Invertebrates form the major part of the food of brook trout, though large individuals become predatory.

Fishing for brook trout

Brook trout are normally caught on flies and have a high reputation as a game fish. The British rod-caught record is 5 lb 13 oz (2.65 kg), caught by Mr A. Pearson at the Avington Fishery, Hants in 1981.

Characteristics

Dorsal fin: 10–14 rays.
Anal fin: 9–13 rays, with a black stripe.
Adipose fin present.
Teeth only on the head of the vomer.
Scales in the lateral line: 110–130.

American brook trout, female, bred for stocking on a fish farm. Photographed 17 November.

American brook trout, male, in spawning colours, bred for stocking on a fish farm. Photographed 17 November.

Craig Pot, a pool on the river Don, Aberdeenshire. The white flowers of sweet cicily in the foreground.

Trout

Trout. *Salmo trutta* Linn. Family *Salmonidae*.
There are two main types of trout native to northern Europe, the brown trout which spends all its life in fresh water and the sea trout which is anadromous and spends some of its life in the sea, before returning to spawn in fresh water.

Brown trout

Brown trout, *S. trutta fario*. French, truite de rivière où de lac; German, Bachforelle, Seeforelle; Swedish, backoring, insjooring; Dutch, beekforel; Finnish, puro taimen, jarvitaimen.

Recognition and related species

No fish is more variable than the brown trout. It can be a silvery fat fish with small black spots, a small thin blackish fish of a few grams with few large red or black spots, or a heavily spotted monster up to 10 kg (20 lb). The combination of spots along the side and an adipose fin distinguish it from fish of other families. Rainbow trout may be distinguished by the numerous small dark spots on their dorsal fin and tail. The differences between salmon and trout are mentioned under salmon, but silvery brown trout are seldom found in waters to which salmon (p.18) or sea trout (p.32) have access. In many areas intermediates are found between sea trout and brown trout. These are called tidal trout, estuarine trout or slob trout and appear to be brown trout which have been feeding in estuaries. They are usually sandy brown with more and heavier spots than sea trout. The famous great trout of Loch Steness in Orkney was one of these; it weighed 13.5 kg (30 lb) when caught on 15 March 1889. Slob trout have been considered a separate species, but are possibly hybrids between brown trout and sea trout, or merely brown trout which have taken advantage of richer feeding in brackish water.
Several subspecies of brown trout are recorded from the continent, notably *S. trutta macrostigma*, with irregular dark blotches, which is found in isolated populations bordering the Mediterranean, in N. Africa, Corsica and Sardinia, southern Greece and the Taurus mountains in Turkey.
Ten other subspecies are found in the eastern Alps, in Yugoslavia and in northern Greece.
The great variability of the brown trout led some authorities in the late 19th century (notably Dr A. C. Gunther), to recognize many separate species. Later authorities (e.g. P. D. Malloch) considered that all the

Brown trout, northern river form, river Don, Aberdeenshire. Photographed 6 June.

Trout parr from river Don, Aberdeenshire, lying on water starwort. Photographed 7 June.

variation was caused by different ecological pressures operating on the same species – that differences in size, shape and colour were produced by different feeding, water chemistry and colour, colour of bottom, etc. Recent studies of blood enzymes by electrophoresis have shown to what extent the differences are ecologically and to what extent genetically determined, and have gone some way to justify those who considered many different species to be able to coexist.

Lough Melvin on the border of Co. Leitrim and Co. Fermanagh is remarkable in that it contains five forms of trout, as well as salmon, charr, perch and minnows, but no pike or other members of the carp family. Some sea trout do come up into the lough but are rare.

A. Ferguson and F. M. Mason (1981) studied four different forms of brown trout which had long been recognized in Lough Melvin, and compared their diet, age, size and general appearance: the sonaghan (*S. nigripinnis* Gunther) has very dark or black fins with elongate pectorals, silvery or dark sides with large black spots and few red spots: 70% of its diet was plankton, mainly *Daphnia*.

The gillaroo (*S. stomachius* Gunther) was golden brown or yellow with many large vivid orange-red spots, especially below the lateral line. The head was small, the body deep; 58% of the diet was molluscs and 27% *Trichoptera* larvae (caddis), and over 500 mollusc shells were found in one fish's stomach. A third group were 'normal' brown trout, not clearly belonging to the other groups; their diet was varied, mainly plankton (57%), *Trichoptera* larvae and *Asellus* (freshwater louse). Finally the ferox trout which had few spots, a large mouth with numerous large teeth, were larger and older than the other groups – they ate mainly char with some *Chaoborous* larvae and *Ephemeroptera* nymphs. The four types spawned separately, though the brown trout and sonaghan spawned in the same stream.

The electrophoretic studies confirmed that the four types are genetically distinct, and estimates of the numbers of years they had been breeding separately were surprising: the ferox had been distinct from the others for 230,000 years, the gillaroo from the sonaghan 65,000 years and from the brown trout 40,000 years. The closest pair were the brown and sonaghan which had probably been isolated for only 5,000 years, or had to some extent been interbreeding. There was indeed some evidence that the brown trout were descendants of Loch Leven trout introduced into Lough Melvin some years ago.

This very long period of reproductive isolation indicates that the different forms of trout in Lough Melvin had entered the lough separately after the last Ice Age, and although living in the same water, have remained distinct ever since.

The recognition of these different types elsewhere is difficult. Sonaghan are known from other areas, notably North Wales. Gillaroos are rare in Ireland, though found in Lough Neagh, and are known from some Sutherland lochs, for example Loch Mulach Corrie. Four forms of trout

were recognized by Col. T. Thornton in 1804 in Loch Laggan, Inverness-shire, on his Sporting Tour of the Highlands, and three forms are known from Fionn Loch in Wester Ross. Ferox are the most ancient and the most widespread of these different trout types. They are known in many places, usually in large deep lakes which also contain char or whitefish. In Scotland they have been recorded from over twenty lochs, all north of the Highland Boundary fault, the most famous of which is probably Loch Rannoch.

In England they are found commonly in the Lake District and they are scattered throughout western Ireland, as well as being recorded in Lough Neagh. They are variable in colour, usually heavily spotted but sometimes silvery and salmon-like. They may be as old as 23 years, but are usually between 10 and 13 years old when caught, and weigh between 3 and 12 kg (6½–25 lb). They grow at the normal rate for the first six years or so, until they reach 30 cm (12 in), and then go over to a diet of char (or sometimes salmon smolts or whitefish), suddenly increasing in weight just as normal trout of the same age are dying. Because of the widespread stocking of brown trout in England most populations are of mixed parentage and not clearly recognizable as distinct types. Loch Leven trout in particular were widely spread around the country because of their fast growth rate, small heads and deep shapely bodies.

Habitat and distribution

Brown trout are common in streams, rivers and lakes. In streams and rivers they will lie in deep runs, in pools and in holes under the bank, moving into shallower water to feed. In lakes they tend to keep to relatively shallow water where the feeding is best, coming to the surface in the evening or during a hatch of flies. Only the large ferox remain at great depth with the char on which they feed. Because of stocking, trout are found in all suitable waters in the British Isles. They require purer water than most fish, with a high oxygen content and relatively low temperature. On the continent trout are found from Spain eastwards to Bulgaria and north to Norway and northern Russia. They are also found in the Caucasus and northern Turkey, east to Afghanistan and the Oxus, and have been introduced into many other parts of the world.

Large lake trout similar to ferox are known from most of the large lakes in the Alps and Carpathians, from many lakes in Scandinavia, and from Iceland, and Newfoundland. Again they live with and prey on charr and whitefish, and all three probably entered these waters after the Ice Age.

Breeding and growth

Trout spawn in autumn and winter on shallows in running water, the female making a redd or small depression in the gravel. In a small stream these redds can be easily seen because the gravel appears paler where it has been disturbed. Big trout can be seen when spawning, their backs

Brown trout, chalk stream form, from river Kennet, Wiltshire, at spawning time. Photographed 22 November.

Brown trout, chalk stream form, from river Kennet, Wiltshire, at spawning time. Photographed 22 November.

Brown trout, form from peaty mountain lake, from Loch Lee, Angus. Photographed 11 June.

29

Loch Arkaig, Inverness-shire.

often out of water. River trout usually move upstream to selected spawning areas, lake trout move into streams.

The ova hatch after one to two months depending on temperature, and the fry usually emerge from the gravel in March. At the end of the first summer they may have reached 15 cm (6 in) if the feeding is good. At this stage they often have parr markings similar to young salmon. Growth is at all stages dependent on food supply.

Some acid lakes, where spawning is easy but food scarce, may contain thousands of small trout under 225 gm (½ lb), others, apparently similar, but with very limited spawning may contain few large specimens up to 2 kg (4½ lb). Alkaline and rather shallow lakes provide ideal conditions for good growth and a stock of fish of a large size. Here a weight of 2–3 kg (4½–6½ lb) may be reached in about seven years. Maximum size depends on many factors; non-ferox brown trout may reach 4.5–6.75 kg (10–15 lb) under natural conditions in Britain, but 22.5 kg (50 lb) specimens have been recorded e.g. in Yugoslavia.

Feeding

Trout are carnivorous but beyond that will eat anything. Some of the differences in diet shown by different types are mentioned above. Most trout, however, feed actively on insects both at larval and adult stage and it is this habit which has led to the development of fly fishing as the most usual way of catching trout. Larger specimens are often actively predatory, taking minnows and other small fish, as well as their own young, when these are available in sufficient numbers.

Fishing for trout

Trout may be caught on nearly all baits, and I know of a pool with several large fish which feed keenly on sliced bread. Many are caught by anglers fishing for other species on maggots and worms, especially when fished in muddy water during a spate. Large trout are mostly caught by spinning, by live-baiting, especially with a minnow or a small trout, or by using minnow-like lures such as a muddler.

It is fly-fishing, however, that has become the most popular way of catching trout, particularly in Britain and America, but also in Europe. The catching of a large fish on a small fly and delicate tackle gives the fisherman the greatest satisfaction, and the deceiving and hooking of a wary trout by imitating the insect on which it is seen to be feeding is the essence of the sport. A knowledge of the habits and species of aquatic insects, or those commonly blown into water, is part of the armoury of the successful dry-fly fisherman. In dry-fly fishing, the fisherman's fly imitates a surface insect, and floats on the water. The adults of two major families are involved, the mayflies (*Ephemeroptera*) and the sedges (*Trichoptera*), as well as several minor families important on still water. In dry-fly fishing on rivers, it is important that the fly should not 'drag', i.e. it should be still relative to the surface and not be pulled across by the action of the current on the line. It is only occasionally, such as in very windy weather, or with a large fly at night, that a dragging fly is likely to catch fish. Brown trout take more slowly than sea trout or rainbows, so the strike, to hook the fish, should be later. In wet-fly fishing, the fisherman's fly imitates a swimming insect larva or a small fish. Brown trout move more deliberately than sea trout or rainbows, so the fly should be fished rather slowly, if it imitates an insect, faster if it imitates a small fish.

The British rod-caught record is 19 lb 9 oz (8.8 kg) caught by J. A. F. Jackson in Loch Quoich in 1978. The Irish record is 26 lb 2 oz (11.8 kg), caught by W. Meares on Lough Ennel in July 1894.

Cooking trout

Most trout make excellent eating, but their quality depends greatly on the type of feeding they have had. Small specimens from acid water usually have white, softer flesh whereas those from alkaline water have firmer, richer pink flesh. Small specimens are best fried or grilled, larger ones may be steamed, boiled and eaten cold. Smoked trout are popular, and they are usually hot-smoked, and therefore cooked, rather than cold-smoked and eaten raw as is smoked salmon.

Characteristics

Dorsal fin: 12–14 rays.
Anal fin: 10–12 rays.
Adipose fin present.
Scales between adipose fin and lateral line: 13–16.

Brown trout, ferox form, from Loch Arkaig. By examination of its scales (p.6) this fish was found to be over 12 years old. Photographed 18 September.

Estuary of river Ythan, Aberdeenshire.

Sea trout

Sea trout, white trout (Ireland); sewin (Wales); finnock (Scotland); whitling blacktail (Tweed). *S. trutta trutta* Linn. French, truite de mer; German, Meerforelle; Swedish, oring; Dutch, zeeforel; Finnish, taimen.

Recognition and related species

When fresh from the sea, sea trout are easily distinguished from brown trout by their silvery bodies with small black spots. After they have been in the river for some weeks, or even months, before spawning, they become darker and blacker or redder as our picture of spawning fish shows, and at this stage they may be difficult to distinguish from brown trout. Most brown trout however have some pink spots and would be likely to have white flesh while sea trout, from their rich feeding in the sea, would still have pink flesh. The distinction is further confused by fast-growing brown trout in rich lakes which are often silvery with black and no red spots, but these are anyway not likely to be confused with sea trout by the fisherman. Such fish, with deep pink flesh, are found in marl-bottomed limestone lakes such as those in central Ireland, or in reservoirs such as Graffham Water in Cambridgeshire.

Sea trout are probably not all of one race, but are sea-going forms of different races of trout that are found in fresh water. Recently it has been suggested by E. Fahy and P. Warren (1984) that large long-lived sea trout are sea-run ferox (p.28). These are found mainly around the east coasts of Scotland, Wales and Ireland, and genetic similarities have been detected between the large sea trout in the Waterville fishery in Co. Kerry and the ferox of Lough Melvin.

Migratory races of trout are also found in the Black Sea and in the Caspian, and these two have been given scientific names, *S. trutta labrax* and *S. trutta caspius* respectively.

The salmon is the fish most closely resembling the sea trout. Hybrids between the two are frequent and sometimes even pure specimens may be difficult to identify, except by modern chemical means; the distinctions are discussed under salmon (p.18).

Habitat and distribution

Sea trout are found in all rivers which are fast flowing and clean enough for them to breed and migrate. The best fisheries are those with ample spawning beds for the adult fish, and lochs close to the sea in which the running fish can rest.

These conditions are found mainly off the west coast of Scotland and Ireland, but excellent sea-trout fisheries are also found in larger rivers often in company with salmon, e.g. the rivers Spey and Tweed in Scotland, and many rivers in Wales. In many cases sea trout may spawn primarily in a particular tributary, salmon in the main river.

In the sea, sea trout do not make the same long journeys as salmon, but stay within the general area up to 200 km (125 miles) in Baltic sea trout of their home river. This has made them less vulnerable to fishing on the high seas, as they tend to remain within territorial waters. Young sea trout have been found to be guided back to their natal stream by scent, but older fish which have returned before are guided more by sight and experience. Even these, if captured and released outside their home range, will be unable to find their way back.

In Europe the sea trout has much the same distribution as the salmon, from northwest Spain northwards to the Arctic Ocean in western Russia, and all round the Baltic. It is also found in southern Iceland and Newfoundland. Successful runs of sea trout have been established in other parts of the world, notably Tierra del Fuego, the Falkland Islands (up to 9 kg/20 lb), and Tasmania.

Breeding and growth

Sea trout enter rivers during the summer. The larger ones, particularly the long-lived variety mentioned above, tend to enter first, in May or even earlier, the smaller ones later, mostly in July or August depending on the amount of water in the rivers, and in dry seasons they will remain in the sea until as late as October.

Spawning takes place from October onwards in gravel in shallow running water in a similar way to brown trout. The fry and parr are similar to those of brown trout, but at about two years old they descend to the sea, becoming smolts, similar to those of salmon. Most of them will have reached the sea by the beginning of June, and in contrast to salmon, many of these return after three or four months as finnock or whitling, weighing 250–500 gm (½–1 lb). These young sea trout probably do not spawn in their first year, but winter in the rivers before returning to the sea in spring. After this they will tend to re-enter the rivers yearly, weighing about 500 g–1 kg (1–2 lb) after the first year and up to 4 kg (9 lb) at the end of a second summer feeding in the sea.

The largest specimens are probably seven to ten years old, but size depends greatly on the richness of the feeding in the sea.

The British record sea trout of 9 kg (20 lb) was caught by Mr G. Leary on 7 November 1983 from the Castle Pool on Tweed at Peebles. Fish of

Sea trout, female at spawning time, from river Lune. Photographed 17 November.

Sea trout, male at spawning time, from river Lune. Photographed 17 November.

Estuary of Iorsa water, Arran.

this size are, however, common in the Baltic, where they may reach 13.5 kg (30 lb).

Feeding

During their stay in the sea sea trout feed on sand eels, sprats and other small fish, and on crustaceans. There has been some controversy as to whether sea trout feed in rivers up which they have come to spawn. There is little doubt that they do, although in many cases not very keenly, and they continue to lose weight until spawning, as do salmon. This is not surprising when the poverty of feeding in most sea-trout rivers is compared with the richness of that in the sea.

Fishing for sea trout

Most of the techniques used for brown trout fishing can also be used for sea trout, but two methods are especially popular, dapping and wet-fly fishing. Dry-fly fishing is less often used, although the specimen shown here was caught on a small dry Greenwells Glory intended for a brown trout.

Sea trout can often be seen leaping in the sea, and, especially in dry seasons, will enter small estuaries in large numbers on the rising tide, jumping and swirling around before dropping back into the sea on the ebb. Under these conditions huge numbers are caught in large estuaries in nets which take both trout and salmon.

In smaller estuaries fishing may be successful, either spinning or using a long lure or a sand eel, but even this fishing is better when the supply of fresh water is good and the river is not very low. In the Shetlands and in other parts of northern Scotland, sea trout are often caught in the sea, using normal wet flies or lures, but further south they seldom seem to take in the sea.

In rivers, sea trout may be caught on wet flies; they tend to lie in the tails of the pools and a wet fly fished fast across them is the most successful; in high water it is advisable to fish more slowly.

Night fishing is also an exciting and productive method at low water. Wet flies, or even dry flies which imitate sedges, are used, and cast out into the darkness of a deep still pool before being retrieved in jerks. The fish can be heard making gigantic splashes all around, and then suddenly they grab the fly. The darker and warmer the night, the better the fishing is supposed to be.

In lakes wet flies are generally used, fished fast from a drifting boat or from the bank. Where three flies are used, the top should be the largest, and be fished as much as possible on the surface, creating a wake in the water. When there is a strong breeze, dapping is a good technique. A long rod is used and a light line which is carried out by the wind; the fly is large and very bushy and bounces over the surface, before being seized by a trout shooting up from the depths.

Cooking sea trout

Sea trout, or salmon trout as they are often called by fishmongers, are excellent eating, as good as salmon, but slightly more delicate.

Large specimens may be cooked or smoked like salmon. Smaller ones can be cut into steaks or filleted, then fried or grilled; they may also be hot-smoked.

Characteristics

Dorsal fin: 12–14 rays.
Anal fin: 10–12 rays.
Adipose fin present.
Scales between adipose fin and lateral line: 13–16.

Sea trout, river Don, Aberdeenshire. Specimen not long up from the sea. Photographed 8 June.

Rutland Water.

Rainbow trout

Rainbow trout, steelhead (migratory race); kamloops (lake race). *Salmo gairdneri* Richardson. Family *Salmonidae*. French, truite arc-en-ciel; German, Regenbogenforelle; Dutch, regenboogforel; Swedish, regnbage; Finnish, kirjoloki.

Recognition and related species

The small black spots which are liberally sprinkled over the tail are a simple way of recognizing the rainbow trout. These are not found in any other trout in Europe. The body is generally silvery with a pinkish zone along either side of the lateral line and both body and fins are also liberally sprinkled with the same small black spots.

Other species of American trout from the west coast have similar small black spots, but they are rarely, if ever, seen in Europe. The cut-throat trout (*S. clarkei*) is also heavily black spotted, often with red on the sides of the head, throat or belly. It reaches 18 kg (40 lb).

The golden trout, a complex group of closely-related species, (e.g. *S. aquabonita*) has golden sides, with a red band, and a golden to yellow belly; the spots are rather large, and the parr marks remain in adults. Maximum size is about 45 cm (18 in).

Habitat and distribution

The rainbow is the most adaptable of trout, both in its native California and in Europe. It lives in lakes, streams and rivers, and many populations feed in the sea, returning to the rivers to spawn. Three main types are found in California, the steelhead which is anadromous, the kamloops, a large, lake form and the rainbow itself which lives in small mountain streams.

Rainbows can thrive in water that would be too warm (up to 22°C/71°F) or too low in oxygen content for brown trout, and this has enabled them to be stocked in small lakes and ponds that were formerly considered suitable only for coarse fish. Because of their hardiness and high growth rate, which has recently been improved still more by selective breeding, rainbows are the most popular fish for intensive raising in fish farms,

both for stocking and for sale frozen or fresh for the table. These farms are usually in fresh water, but may be in brackish water, e.g. the Baltic and even in the sea.

The native distribution of the rainbow trout is on the Pacific coast of North America from northern Mexico in the south to Alaska and Canada in the north as far as the Peace and Athabasca rivers. It is also found on the eastern side of the Pacific in Japan and the Soviet far east.

Around 1880 it became possible to transport fertilized trout ova for long distances, and since then rainbows have been widely distributed around the world, e.g. to Australia, New Zealand (1883), South America, southern and east Africa, and to southern Asia as well as throughout Europe and eastern North America.

Rainbow trout were first introduced into Europe in 1882. The ova came from anadromous parents from the McCloud river, a tributary of the Sacramento river in northern California. These are spring spawning and have a strong migratory instinct, so they proved unsuitable for permanent stocking of running water or lakes out of which they could easily escape to the sea.

They were, however, very successful in rich reservoirs such as Blagdon in Somerset, which were then newly made, and have continued to do very well in these lowland waters as is shown by the success of Graffham and Rutland Water today.

Very few breeding populations of rainbow trout are established in England, but they are said to breed successfully in some rivers, notably the Wye in Derbyshire and the Chess in Buckinghamshire.

It has been reported recently that rainbows, which had entered the river from the sea, steelheads, have been caught in the river Test in Hampshire. Conditions for spawning there would seem to be good enough, but these are probably merely stocked fish or escapes from trout farms which had gone down to the sea to feed.

Breeding and growth

Steelheads enter the rivers of California in winter and spawn in early spring. This behaviour is probably linked to the Mediterranean (dry summer) climate where the rivers are very low all summer and the

Rainbow trout. Male from river Kennet, Wiltshire. Photographed 22 November.

Rainbow trout parr, river Chess. Photographed 8 May.

autumn rain often does not come until November. In addition the warmer climate of California enables even spring-spawned fry to make good growth before winter. Autumn spawning is a characteristic of northern or alpine fish which have to contend with a short summer growing season and so benefit by a really early start. Some autumn-spawning strains have been bred in hatcheries.

Rainbow trout spawn in redds cut in gravel by the female, in a manner generally similar to salmon (p.18). Growth can be very fast, and under semi-natural conditions fish have reached over 3.6 kg (8 lb) in four years. In America, steelheads can reach over 16 kg (35 lb) in weight. Kamloops have been recorded up to 23.6 kg (52 lb) but are usually around 3 kg (6–8 lb). The British rod-caught record stands at present at about 9 kg (20 lb), but larger ones are being produced by selective breeding and this record will probably soon be broken.

Feeding

Rainbow trout feed mainly on aquatic invertebrates, such as insect larvae, crustaceans and molluscs. Larger specimens readily eat small fish, in North America shiners, in England perch fry and sticklebacks, and they will enter quite shallow water in pursuit of them. It has been found that they tend to attack isolated fish at the edge of a shoal, which may be slower than the others or disabled in some way.

In rivers they behave in much the same way as brown trout. In still waters they tend to swim in shoals, often moving at some speed and feeding on the surface.

Fishing for rainbows

The same methods as will catch brown trout can also be used for rainbows. Fly-fishing is by far the most popular method, though stray specimens are often caught on maggots and other baits by match fisherman, furious by having their time wasted playing a lively rainbow on delicate match tackle. Even bread can be a successful bait once trout have become accustomed to eating it. Nowadays in England fishing for rainbows has become synonymous with reservoir fishing. Traditional wet flies fished fast from a drifting boat are less productive than lures fished very deep when the water is cold or near the surface or in the shallows in warm weather. These lures imitate the small fish which are a favourite prey for large specimens. Both dry fly and nymph fishing can also be productive when the fish are seen to be taking small duck-flies or sedges on or near the surface. In both cases bank fishing or fishing from

an anchored boat are better methods against cruising rainbows than the traditional drift.

Rainbows have long been credited with excellent memories, so that it may be advisable to use lures which are not familiar to them, but at the same time resemble a likely prey. In a small pond we have found that after two or three have been caught, the others soon learn to ignore all sorts of fly and even to distinguish between free-floating trout pellets and those containing a hook. Bass have been demonstrated to retain this hook-shy behaviour for six months and rainbow trout seem equally able to learn and remember.

When hooked, rainbows fight hard, usually leaping clear of the water and making spectacular long runs.

The British rod-caught record is 19 lb 8 oz (8.844 kg) caught by Mr A. Pearson at the Avington Fishery, Hants, in 1977.

Cooking rainbow trout

A large rainbow trout which has had good feeding can be very similar to a salmon, though with paler, softer flesh. They can even be cold smoked as is traditional for salmon. Smaller specimens are good when hot smoked or eaten in the same way as brown trout, fried or grilled whole or when larger, as cutlets. Very small specimens, *c.*15 cm (6 in) are also very good and this may be the common size in small nutrient-poor streams, e.g. at high altitudes in the tropics.

Characteristics

Anal fin: 10 rays or less; spotted.
Dorsal fin: 11–12 rays.
Adipose fin present, spotted.
Teeth along shaft of vomer.
Scales along the lateral line: 120–150.

Rainbow trout from small silty pond. Photographed 18 April.

Schelly or Gwyniad, Lake Bala. Photographed 11 May.

Schelly, or Gwyniad

Schelly, gwyniad (Wales) *Coregonus nilssoni* Valenciennes syn.
C. perinanti Valenciennes. Family *Coregonidae*. Swedish, planktonsik;
German, kleine Schwebranke: Austria, Felchen.

Recognition and related species

The schelly and other whitefish are easy to recognize by their
combination of an unmarked silvery body with the adipose fin
characteristic of the salmon family. Smelts (p.134) are rather similar (and
the whitefish also are said by some to smell of cucumber), but have
greenish, almost translucent bodies and conspicuous sharp teeth.
Grayling are easily distinguished by their very large dorsal fins, marked
with red.

It is when the scientist tries to distinguish the different species of
whitefish that the difficulties start, and the genus *Coregonus* has been
called 'a *crux et skandalon* for taxonomists, but a challenge to
evolutionists'. As with trout, different populations may coexist in the
same lake, some remaining distinct species, some hybridizing to form
intermediates. Not only have repeated invasions from east and west after
the Ice Ages brought different closely related species together, but
movement of useful forms by man has been going on in Scandinavia for
several hundred years, usually to introduce fast growing species to lakes
where only small species were formerly known. Similar movements, to
the confusion of taxonomists, have taken place in the Alpine lakes in
Austria, Switzerland, and northern Italy. Indeed it is said that there are
no pure populations left in the Alps.

These fish have been studied in detail, especially in Sweden by Svardson
and the species mentioned here are based on the account he published in
1979. Four groups of species are recognized in Europe.

1. Peled group, including *C. nilssoni* (the Schelly), *C. wartmanni* (the
   Powen, p.43) and the northern *C. pallasi*.
2. Pidschian group, including *C. lavaretus* (above), *C. acronius* and
   C. fera.
3. *Coregonus autumnalis pollan* (the Pollan, p.43).
4. Vendace group (p.42).

Lake Bala, north Wales.

Habitat and distribution

The peled itself (*C. pallasi*) is mainly an Arctic species found in the
Baltic and on the Arctic coast of Sweden, Russia and Siberia. It can reach
a weight of 5 kg (11 lb) and spawns both in rivers and lakes after a long
migration.

The schelly or gwyniad is found in Lake Bala in Wales and in Red Tarn,
Haweswater and Ullswater in the Lake District. It probably survived
the more recent Ice Ages to the west of the ice sheet which covered

Scandinavia and the Baltic and entered the British lakes when the Irish
sea was in fresh water. Later it colonized Lake Constance, and
Thunersee near Berne from the Rhine, and Denmark from the North
Sea area.

Breeding and growth

Spawning takes place in December and January, the eggs being laid over

Houting, a land-locked form, from a lake near Ruovesi, Finland. Photographed 26 June.

gravel or stones in moderately deep water. Adult length is about 20–30 cm (8–12 in).

Feeding
The stomachs of specimens taken in May in Lake Bala contained mostly small worms, probably midge larvae, but also tiny molluscs, crustaceans and some adult midges. These suggest that it feeds on the surface as well as on the bottom.

Fishing for schelly
Schelly are not commonly caught by fishermen, though a small maggot fished deep has been successful on Lake Bala, and bloodworms on a tiny hook should also prove effective. The specimens we photographed were taken in a gill net by fishery scientists.

Cooking schelly
All whitefish are excellent to eat. The specimens we cooked had firm, white and rich flesh and were excellent grilled, every bit as good as a sardine.

Characteristics
Dorsal fin: 14–15 rays.
Anal fin: 10–12 rays.
Adipose fin present.
Scales along the lateral line: 73–90.

Houting
Houting, river spawning whitefish. *Coregonus lavaretus* Linn. Syn *C. oxyrhinchus* Linn. Family *Coregonidae*. French, bondelle; German, Schnapel; Swiss, gangfisch; Swedish, sik; Finnish, siika, jarvisiika.

Recognition and related species
The houting is distinguished from other whitefish by its very long snout, with the upper jaw projected well beyond the lower; the exact length of the snout varies, but it may be twice the diameter of the eye.

Habitat and distribution
The houting is usually found in fresh or brackish water during winter and spring and migrates to the sea in summer to feed. There are, however, some entirely land-locked populations in the Alps and in Scandinavia living in large lakes, e.g. Lake Vanern in southern Sweden. Few houting have ever been seen in the British Isles. Formerly they were reported along the south east coast, around East Anglia, and these may have been stray specimens from the Rhine. The North Sea population is now probably extinct, owing to the pollution of the Weser, Elbe and Rhine, in which it used to run up as far as Strasbourg.
In the Baltic it is still a common and important commercial fish, both in the Neva in Russia and in Finnish and Swedish rivers running into the Gulfs of Bothnia and Finland.

Breeding and growth
Houting begin their spawning migration in August moving into the rivers to spawn in October and November, when the water temperature has fallen to about 5°C (41°F). The eggs are laid over fine gravel in running water.
The young descend to the sea as fry, moving to the feeding areas which may be as much as 700 km (450 miles) from the river mouth, but are often nearer.
The maximum recorded size is about 70 cm (28 in) and a weight of 10 kg (22 lb), but a length of 50 cm (20 in) and weight of 2 kg (4 lb) is more usual.

Feeding
The houting is probably mainly a bottom feeder, searching with its snout for worms, molluscs and crustaceans in the mud.

Fishing for houting
Few houting are caught on rod and line, but some are recorded as caught both through the ice in winter and in summer in lakes. Small earthworms, maggots, or bloodworms would make suitable bait. Gill netting is the most commonly used method of catching houting, both in the sea and in fresh water.

Cooking houting
Houting are excellent to eat, either grilled, baked whole in foil, or hot-smoked in the manner of trout. The flesh is white, firm and slightly oily, a little firmer than that of a herring.

Characteristics
Dorsal fin: 14–15 rays.
Anal fin: 13–16 rays.
Adipose fin present.

Lake Myllylahti, Finland

Vendace *(illustrated p.43)*

Vendace. *Coregonus vandesius* Richardson. Family *Coregonidae*. Other names (or for *C. albula* Linn.). French, petite marêne; German, kleine Marane; Swedish, sikloja; Finnish, miukku.

Recognition and related species

The vendace is the smallest of the European whitefish, and easily distinguished from the other species by its strongly curved lower jaw which protrudes upwards to meet the short upper jaw. Its eye is large; its body silvery with a blue sheen on the sides, dark greyish on the back, with very delicate and easily removed scales. The western European vendace, *C. vandesius* is distinguished by Svardson, from the eastern European *C. albula* which is the common species in the Baltic. A third European species, *C. trybonii*, differs by being spring-spawning.

Habitat and distribution

Most vendace live in clear cool lakes, swimming in shoals in middle water, but some large forms inhabit very deep water, usually below 15 m (45 ft). Some are also found in the sea in less saline areas of the Baltic and in the lower reaches of the large rivers of Siberia.

The western *C. vandesius* is found in the Lake District in England in Derwentwater and Bassenthwaite and was formerly found in Castle Loch at Loch Maben in Dumfries and Galloway region. It is now extinct in Castle Loch owing to eutropification by the town's sewage; it may possibly still survive in Mill Loch nearby. On the Continent, *C. vandesius* has been found in France, in the Lac de Chauvet, and in north-west Germany eastwards to Mecklenberg where, in some small lakes, both *C. vandesius* and *C. albula* live together.

C. albula is much commoner, being found all round the Baltic, from Denmark to Finland, central Poland and northern Russia. It is found in brackish water in the northern and eastern parts of the Baltic, the gulfs of Finland and Bothnia.

Breeding and growth

Spawning takes place in shallow water over gravel in early winter, the Baltic populations entering rivers to spawn from September onwards. Vendace are usually small, between 10 and 25 cm (4 and 12 in), but the larger forms from deep cold lakes may reach 1.2 kg (2½ lb). Maximum age is six to seven years.

Feeding

The small forms feed on plankton. Specimens from a lake in central Finland contained mostly *Daphnia* with some mosquitoes, both larvae and winged adults. The large forms are often fish-eating or live on molluscs and larger crustacea.

Fishing for vendace

Because of their small size and planktonic diet, small vendace are hardly ever caught on a rod and line, but in special fine-mesh gill nets. Some idea of their importance in Scandinavia may be seen from the fact that in Finland the vendace is the second or third most common freshwater fish species caught (after perch and pike). In the Lake District it seems that the vendace was never commonly caught, but in the 19th century in Loch Maben there were two clubs devoted to catching and feasting on vendace, the Vendace Club for Gentry and the St Magdalene Vendace Club, 'an organization of a very decided democratic kind'; both of them seem to have been wound up in about 1870, due to scarcity of the fish.

Cooking vendace

Vendace are delicious either grilled, preferably over an open fire, or fried. Smaller specimens can be eaten whole, heads, bones and all, after the manner of the whitebait. They are also salted and eaten as an appetizer, but these are distinctly an acquired taste.

Larger specimens are good cooked in the same way as large sardines which they resemble in size and shape, though vendace are less scaly. The flesh is firm and tasty.

Characteristics

Dorsal fin: 11 rays. Anal fin: 13 rays.
Adipose fin present. Scales along the lateral line: 68–71.

Vendace, Lake Myllylahti. Our specimen damaged in netting. Photographed 29 June.

Pollan (*not illustrated*)

Pollan *Coregonus autumnalis pollan* Thompson. Family *Coregonidae*.

Recognition and related species
The pollan is the species of whitefish found in some Irish loughs. It is interesting that recent electrophoretic studies on the blood proteins have confirmed that Tate Regan's remarks on the species, made in 1911 in *British Freshwater Fishes*, were correct, though ignored by many later authors. The pollan 'is not very different from an Arctic marine species which enters the rivers of Siberia; but there are no Europan whitefish at all closely related to it'.
The pollan is intermediate between the vendace and the other whitefish, and possibly arose from a hybrid between the two before the last Ice Age. Specimens are difficult to tell from vendace unless their lake of origin is known, but *C. autumnalis* is an Arctic anadromous species found all round the Arctic Ocean in Alaska and northwest Canada to Bathurst Inlet, and in eastern Siberia. A land-locked population has also survived in Lake Baikal. It was perhaps one of the earliest migrants into western Europe after the last retreat of ice about 10,000 years ago and colonized Ireland via the Shannon, the first area to emerge from the ice.

Habitat and distribution
The pollan has been found in Lough Neagh where it formerly supported an important fishery and was exported to north-western England. It is also known from Loughs Erne, both Upper and Lower, Lough Ree and Lough Derg on the Shannon.

Breeding and growth
Although *C. autumnalis* itself spawns in rivers, the Irish pollan spawns in open water on the bottom of the lake in winter. Growth is probably slow.
Specimens from the Arctic have been recorded between eleven and twenty years old. The pollan usually reaches about 25 cm (10 in) in length, and a weight of 170 gm (6 oz), though specimens of 1.2 kg (2½ lb) were recorded in the past from Lough Neagh.

Feeding
Mainly planktonic crustaceans such as *Daphnia longispina* in Lough Derg and *Mysis relicta* in Lough Neagh, and small insects.

Characteristics
Dorsal fin: 13 or 14 rays.
Anal fin: 12 or 13 rays.
Adipose fin present.
Scales in the lateral line: 74–86.

Powan (*illustrated p. 7*)

Powan. *Coregonus wartmanni* Bloch, syn *C. clupeoides* Lacepêdè. Family *Coregonidae*. German, Blaufelchen; Swedish, blasik.

Recognition and related species
The powan is very similar to the schelly but differs in usually having fewer gill rakers (usually thirty-six), but only experts could distinguish the two if they did not know from which lake they came!

Habitat and distribution
The powan is a subarctic fish living in lakes in northern Europe, in the Alps and the Carpathians. It swims in shoals which take a regular route, grazing on the plankton as they go.
In the British Isles the powan is found only in Loch Lomond and nearby Lock Eck. On the Continent they are commoner than the schelly, being found in the Alps in about twenty-five lakes, and in south Sweden, south Norway, Finland and western Russia.

Breeding and growth
In Loch Lomond spawning takes place in early January, the eggs being laid on to banks of gravel or boulders off headlands, and on to reefs in the middle of the loch. Adult size is 20–30 cm (10–12 in), reached in three to four years, but specimens of around 1 kg (2 lb) and 42 cm (16 in) and as old as ten years are recorded.
The Blaufelchen in Lake Constance are said to spawn over deep water, the eggs slowly falling to the bottom where they develop through the winter.

Feeding
Planktonic crustacea, mainly *Bosmina*, *Daphnia* and *Cyclops*, form the major diet from May to September. Chironomid larvae are eaten also in August and September. In early winter they feed mainly on the bottom, on *Asellus*, the freshwater louse, and water snails.
Specimens we examined from Lake Pyhajarvi in Finland in July contained about 90% *Daphnia* with some mosquito larvae and adults.

Fishing for powan
Powan were formerly caught in large numbers in nets in Loch Lomond, and are also sometimes taken there by fly-fishermen or on maggots. We found them excellent eating, white-fleshed and more delicate than a trout.

Characteristics
Dorsal fin: 11 rays. Anal fin: 9–11 rays.
Adipose fin present. Scales in the lateral line: 82.

River Test, Hampshire, the doyen of chalk streams.

Grayling

Grayling. *Thymallus thymallus* Linn. Family *Thymallidae*. French, ombre commun; German, Asche; Swedish, harr; Finnish, harjus.

Recognition and related species
The grayling is a distinct and elegant fish, easily recognized by its large dorsal fin, edged with brownish-red. In its small adipose fin it is similar to trout and salmon, but its silvery body and large scales are more like those of a roach or chub. There are no other fish related to the grayling in western Europe, though there are two other species in Siberia and Mongolia, and one in the Canadian Arctic.

Habitat and distribution
The grayling shares many of its habitat requirements with the trout. It favours clean, clear, well-oxygenated water, especially richer streams with good weed growth and a gravelly or sandy bottom. It is found throughout England and southern Scotland, being especially common in the chalk streams of Hampshire and Dorset, in the Severn and the Wye, in Yorkshire, in the Tweed, the Nith and neighbouring rivers. It is also common in parts of the Tay and its tributaries the Isla and the Earn; it is recorded that it was introduced here in the 1880s.
On the Continent grayling are found in the Alps and Carpathians northwards to western Russia and Scandinavia.

Breeding and growth
The grayling spawns from March to May, among sand and gravel in running water. The eggs are yellow, 3.6 mm (⅛ in) in diameter, and laid in a shallow redd made by the female. They are very prolific fish, and many thousands are netted out of chalk streams, such as the Test and the Kennet, every year, without any long-term effect on the population.

Mature grayling average about 340 gm (12 oz) in most British rivers and a 1 kg (2 lb) specimen is a good one. Grayling grow very quickly, reaching about 30 cm (12 in) in three years. The present British rod-caught record stands at 1.645 kg (3 lb 10 oz), caught by Mr I. White in 1983 from the river Allen, Dorset, but several fish over 2 kg (4 lb) have been caught. On the Continent specimens over 60 cm (2 ft) and 2.5 kg (5 lb) have been reported.

Feeding
The grayling has a small soft mouth, and feeds mainly on aquatic larvae, nymphs and small worms and crustacea. They also regularly take surface flies.

Fishing for grayling
The same methods as are used for trout will usually catch grayling. Small dry flies and nymphs are usually successful, as are wet flies such as partridge and orange, red tag, or the appropriately named Grayling Witch. Small worms are good as bait, if the weather is cold and fish are not rising.
A grayling which can be seen lying in the water can sometimes be induced to take by being cast over repeatedly with the fly. The rise is usually quicker and more splashy than that of a trout. When hooked, grayling fight well, using their large dorsal fins for leverage in the current; because of their soft mouths they have to be played gently. Grayling make good eating, but are usually unjustly neglected, though some prefer them to trout. The flesh is white and firm. Grayling reach their best condition after the end of the trout season, from October onwards through the winter until they spawn.

Characteristics
Dorsal fin: 17–24 rays. Anal fin: 13–16 rays. Adipose fin present.

Grayling, river Test, Hampshire; with leaves of comfrey. Photographed 6 October.

Minnows, river Ouvézè, Ardèche, France. Females ready to spawn. Photographed 18 May.

Minnow

Minnow. *Phoxinus phoxinus* Linn. Family *Cyprinidae*. French, vairon, cuzean; German, Elritze; Swedish, kvidd; Finnish, mutu.

Recognition and related species

The minnow is the smallest member of the carp family native to the British Isles. It is a slender fish with no barbels, a brown and greenish barred back and sides, giving the appearance of a black stripe along the flank, and pale brownish fins. A dark spot on the 'wrist' of the tail is a distinctive feature. Intensity of colour varies greatly, both with the colour of the water and the background (in very cloudy water the fish are pale and almost unmarked) and with the mood of the fish; they may lose much of their colour when alarmed. The scales are very small. It is unlikely to be confused with any other fish: the stone loach and the gudgeon both have similar colouring, but they have barbels at the mouth and the characteristic flat underside of bottom-living fish.
Two other species of minnow are found in Europe, both in the far northeast. The swamp minnow (*P. percnurus*) and the poznan minnow (*P. czekanowskii*). Both are distinct, with golden brown liberally spotted sides, and red fins.

Habitat and distribution

The minnow is found in shoals in clear lakes, small fast-flowing streams and fast rivers, from the mountains down to sea level in the north. Generally it favours rather clean water and tends to keep in shallows or close to weeds near the edge, for its own protection against larger fish. It is common from Ireland and lowland Scotland, south to the Pyrenees, and the Rhone to the Balkans, the eastern coast of the Black Sea and across Siberia to Kamchatka.

Breeding and growth

Minnows spawn from April to mid-July, laying their adhesive eggs over stones in the shallows. The eggs remain in a mass, and stick to the stones.

At the spawning season the male becomes reddish on the throat and belly; the female becomes distended with spawn, her belly shining silver; females are larger than males. Adult length is 6–10 cm (2½–4 in) and 14 cm (5½ in) is about the maximum length reached.

Feeding

Minnows are omnivorous, eating mostly small worms, insect larvae and crustaceans.

Fishing for minnow

Minnows are seldom caught for their own value, but as bait for larger species such as trout. They are easily caught on small worms and maggots fished near the bottom, or, if required in quantity, in a shallow net which can be laid on the bottom suitably baited either with food or with something small and red such as a piece of wool which will attract them.

Cooking minnow

Minnows were formerly highly regarded in England and Scotland and served in huge numbers at State banquets, e.g. at a great banquet given at Winchester by William of Wykeham to Richard II and Queen Anne. They were also made into a tansy, a sort of omelette made with yolk of eggs and flavoured with cowslips, primroses and tansy (compare with elvers p.122).
A method more suitable to the modern palate would be to treat them as whitebait and fry them until crisp, but care should be taken to ensure that they come from reasonably unpolluted water and are well gutted before being cooked.

Characteristics

Dorsal fin: 9–10 rays.
Anal fin: 9–10 rays.
Scales in the lateral line: 80–100.
Pharyngeal teeth: 5 and 2 very thin in two rows.

Weir on river Loddon, Hampshire.

Stone loach from East Stour, Kent, with water crowfoot. Photographed 14 July.

Stone loach

Stone loach. *Noemacheilus barbatulus* Linn. Family *Cobitidae*. French, loche franche; German, Schmerle; Swedish, grönling.

Recognition and related species
This small, slender bottom-living fish is commonly found in clear stony or sandy streams. There are only two loaches found in the British Isles; both appear scaleless, have elongated bodies and rounded fins, variously mottled. The stone loach has six long barbels, rather uneven in length, and more than eleven rays in the pectoral fins. The spined loach has shorter equal barbels and less than nine rays in the pectoral fins, a spine below each eye, and is found much more rarely, in deeper and more sluggish water. The two species are most easily distinguished in the field by their body profile; the stone loach is cylindrical and flattened on the belly, as would be expected of a bottom-living fish, whereas the spined loach is laterally flattened. The gudgeon is similar in general habits and appearance to the stone loach, but has a much more forked tail and conspicuous scales, as well as having only one pair of barbels.

Habitat and distribution
While sandy or stony streams are its usual habitat, especially in the lowlands, the stone loach is also found in shallow pebbly stretches of rivers, in gravelly lakes, and in brackish water in the Baltic. It hides under stones or weed by day, or lies motionless, relying on camouflage for protection. It is often found in large streams with dace and chub, but also in smaller streams which contain only sticklebacks and the occasional eel or trout.

In the British Isles it is found everywhere except in the mountains and in Northern Scotland and the Isles. On the Continent it is common throughout central Europe, eastwards to North China and the Pacific.

Breeding and growth
Loach spawn in spring, from April to June, laying their eggs among weeds or stones. The usual adult size is around 10 cm (4 in) but exceptionally they reach a length of 15 cm (6 in) and an age of about seven years.

Feeding
Loach feed mainly on invertebrates, small crustacea, larvae and worms.

Fishing for loach
Loach are a common quarry of small boys and girls, usually in small streams, where they can be caught easily by gently driving them into a net which is hidden on the bottom. The specimens shown here were found lying under a large patch of water crowfoot; they stayed still when the weed was slowly parted to one side.

Characteristics
Dorsal fin: 9–10 rays. Anal fin: 6–7 rays.
Barbels around mouth: 6. Scales minute.

East Stour, Kent.

River Box, Suffolk.

Bullhead or Miller's Thumb

Bullhead, miller's thumb or cull. *Cottus gobio* Linn. Family *Cottidae*.
French, chabot; German, Groppe; Dutch, rivierdonderpad; Swedish,
stensimpa.

Recognition and related species

The bullhead is a small fish with a large head and mouth and a tapering
body. It lives on the bottom, hiding under stones or other cover by day,
and emerging to feed at night. It is only likely to be confused with the
stone loach, which occurs in the same type of habitat, but has a slender
head and small mouth ringed with barbels. The bullhead is also
characterized by its two contiguous spiny dorsal fins and large pectorals.
The common goby also sometimes occurs in fresh water (p.136).

Habitat and distribution

The bullhead is found in all rivers and streams with a suitable bottom,
and is also common in stony lakes. In general, clear shallow water with
rich feeding and a pebbly bottom is its favourite habitat.
It is common throughout England and Wales, but rare in Scotland and
found only in the lowlands. It appears to be absent from Ireland. On the
Continent it is found from southern Sweden to northern Spain, to the
Alps, the northern Balkans and western Russia.

Breeding and growth

The bullhead spawns from March onwards; in southern England each
pair may spawn several times during the summer, while in the north, in
colder rivers, they spawn once only. The pinkish eggs are attached in a
lump to the base of a large stone, and are guarded by the male (which
may be distinguished by its smaller mouth) until they hatch, usually in
three to four weeks. They live for at the most four years, and reach a
maximum of 17 cm (6¾ in), though 8–10 cm (3–4 in) is the usual length.

Feeding

Bullheads feed mainly on bottom-living invertebrates such as freshwater
shrimps, and insect larvae such as *Trichoptera* (caddis) and
Chironomidae. They are often accused of eating the eggs of trout and
salmon, since they are found near the redds, but they are probably no
more destructive than small trout or salmon parr themselves.

Fishing for bullheads

Bullheads are easily caught when large stones are carefully lifted up to
reveal them lying underneath, and they can be driven into a net. They
are said to be edible and even good to eat, but I have never felt inclined
to try one, and it would not be easy to get sufficient to make a good meal!

Characteristics

1st dorsal fin: 6–8 spines. 2nd dorsal fin: 15–17 rays.
Anal fin: 13 rays. Lateral line complete.

Siberian bullhead *(not illustrated)*

Siberian bullhead. *Cottus poecilopus* Heckel. Family *Cottidae*. German,
sibirische Groppe; Swedish, bergsimpa; Finnish, kirjoevasimppu.

Recognition and related species

The Siberian bullhead is very similar to the common bullhead, but
differs in having longer pelvic fins, which reach as far as the anus, a
lateral line which ends short of the tail, and one ray of the pelvic fin
which is less than half as long as the other rays.

Habitat and distribution

Found in streams, rivers and lakes, especially in the hills, in Sweden, in
parts of eastern Europe, especially in the Baltic basin, and from
southern Finland across Russia into Siberia. Some authorities consider
the Russian and Siberian form to be distinct.

Breeding, growth and feeding

Similar to the common bullhead. A nest is made in spring under a stone
and the eggs laid there.

Characteristics

1st dorsal fin: 6–8 spines. 2nd dorsal fin: 15–17 rays.
Anal fin: 13 rays. Lateral line incomplete.

Bullheads from East Stour, Kent, on roots of Alder. Photographed 14 July.

Bullhead, from estuary of river Thames at West Thurrock. Photographed 26 October.

Brook lamprey from river Loddon, Hampshire. Photographed 11 November

Brook lamprey

Brook lamprey. *Lampetra planeri* Bloch. Family *Petromyzonidae*.
French, petite lamproie; German, Bachneunauge; Dutch, beek prik;
Swedish, bäcknejonöga.

Recognition and related species
Lampreys are distinguished from other fish by their eel-like bodies,
round, sucker-like mouths, very poorly developed fins, and rows of
breathing holes instead of gills. The eel, which is a similar general shape,
has a normal fish-type mouth, small gills, and properly developed, if
small, pectoral fins.
The brook lamprey is the smallest, and the only one, of the three species
in north-west Europe which spends all its life in fresh water. It is not
easy to distinguish from the other species, but its two dorsal fins are
continuous, whereas in the sea lamprey and the lampern (*L. fluviatilis*)
there is a short gap between the two dorsal fins. There are also small
differences in the mouth structure of the three species.

Habitat and distribution
The brook lamprey is usually found in small streams. The larvae, often
called 'prides', remain buried in soft mud, while the adults are found in
swifter water, especially at spawning time. The brook lamprey is found
throughout north-western Europe and in some parts of the
Mediterranean. It is recorded in scattered localities throughout the
British Isles but is rarely seen, probably because it is nocturnal.

Breeding and growth
The brook lamprey spawns from April to June in sandy and gravelly
areas of streams, making a nest among the stones. It is not known how
long they remain in the larval stage. Adult brook lampreys are 13–25 cm
(5–10 in) long.

Feeding
The larvae feed on minute organisms filtered from the mud; the adults
are supposed not to feed at all.

Fishing for brook lampreys
Because they are so small, brook lampreys are probably never fished for.
They do not have the culinary properties of the other species.

Lampern or River Lamprey *(not illustrated)*

Lampern, river lamprey. *Lampetra fluviatilis* Linn. Family
Petromyzonidae. French, lampoire de rivière; German, Flussneunauge;
Dutch, rivierprik; Swedish, flodréjonöga.

Recognition and related species
The lampern is very similar to the brook lamprey but is larger, the adults
being 30–50 cm (12–20 in) long. The two dorsal fins are distinctly
separate. The sea lamprey (*Petromyzon marinus*, Linn.) differs in being
even larger and yellowish green, mottled with black or brown on the
back. Its mouth structure, especially the arrangement of the teeth, is
different from that of the lampern. The teeth are numerous (about 100)
and arranged in radiating rows all round the disk, those on the upper
side being larger and often paired. It is anadromous and similar to the
lampern in general life cycle. In the sea, it feeds on fish such as salmon,
sea trout, basking sharks, etc., the sucker remaining fixed in one place
while the teeth revolve and rasp into the flesh of the victim. It is frequent
in European and North Atlantic waters, and managed to enter the Great
Lakes in North America via the St Lawrence seaway, causing great
damage to the salmonid stock.
When sea lampreys enter the river to spawn they are 60–90 cm
(24–36 in) long and weigh 2–2.5 kg (2–3 lb). The eggs are laid in a nest,
excavated by both male and female, among stones in running water. The
larvae live in the mud in rivers for a few years before migrating to the sea
to begin feeding on fish.

Habitat and distribution
Adult lamperns migrate from the sea into rivers to spawn, the main
migration starting in autumn after the first heavy rains. By the spawning
time of April–May they are found on stony shallows.

River Coln, Essex.

In the British Isles the lampern is distinctly rare, but scattered throughout the country. Their numbers have been reduced by pollution of estuaries and by weirs, but they seem to be found still particularly commonly on the rivers Dee and Clwyd in North Wales, and around Lough Neagh (Maitland 1972).

On the Continent the lampern is found throughout western Europe except the far north, and all round the Baltic.

Breeding and growth

Spawning takes place in April and May when small shoals of adults (ten to fifty) gather on a stony shallows in running water and lay their eggs among stones. The small fish are worm-like when they hatch, and are so different from the parents that they were formerly called *Ammocoetes branchialis*. These larvae are blind and toothless and live in the mud for three to five years when they metamorphose into adults and migrate to the sea, usually at 15–24 cm (6–8 in) long. It is not known how long they remain in the sea, but one year only is likely, as they are capable of fast growth. On their return to the river they are 30–50 cm (12–20 in) long.

Feeding

At the larval stage, they feed on small organisms filtered from the mud.

At the adult stage in the sea they feed on other fish, attaching themselves by their suckers and boring into the flesh with their rasping teeth.

Fishing for lamperns

The lampern was once a popular table fish and the subject of a profitable fishery at Gloucester on the Severn, and around Hampton Court and Teddington on the Thames; surprisingly most of these seem to have been sold not for eating but as bait to cod and turbot fishermen in the North Sea.

Cooking lamperns

Lamperns were very popular as food fish, and it was probably these, and not the larger, oilier sea lamprey that were the downfall of Henry I. Lamperns can be cooked and put in aspic to make the filling of the traditional lamprey pie, or else made into a ragout. Elizabeth David mentions a wonderful sounding dish from the Bordelais, 'lampoire aux poireaux et au vin rouge'.

Smoked lamprey is delicious, and a popular delicacy in Finland and other parts of the Continent. The flavour is excellent, the texture slightly rubbery and the head, tail, bones, indeed the whole fish is soft enough to eat.

53

River Baume, Ardèche, France.

Apron

Apron or Rhône Streber. *Zingel asper* Linn. Family *Percidae*. Local names: dauphin, sorcier (Rhône); varlet, anadelo (Provence); roi poisson (Saône).

Recognition and related species

Both in habits and general appearance the apron resembles a large and elongated miller's thumb. Its head is longer and narrower in side view and flattened from above. Its pectoral fins are small, but its ventral fins are large and well developed.

It is, however, a member of the perch family which has adapted to life on the bottom of swift-flowing rivers and its similarities with the miller's thumb are examples of convergent evolution in response to life in a similar habitat, in the same way that the similarities between pike and zander have evolved in response to their predatory diet.

Two very similar species are found in eastern Europe, in the Danube basin, the streber (*Zingel streber*) and the zingel (*Zingel zingel*). The streber differs from the apron mainly in having a more slender and elongated caudal peduncle (the part of the body between the second dorsal and anal fins, and the tail). Apart from the Danube it is found in the Vadar river in north-eastern Greece. The zingel is a larger fish (up to 48 cm/19 in) and differs primarily in having more spiny rays in its first dorsal fin, 13–15 as opposed to 8–9 in the apron: the second dorsal fin also has more rays. The zingel is said to inhabit shallows, the streber deeper water.

Habitat and distribution

The apron is known only from the Rhône basin where it is becoming increasingly rare and is seldom seen. In Switzerland it is thought to be now found only in the river Doubs; in France it has been reported from the Ain, Ardèche, Saône, Isère and Durance as well as the Doubs. Our specimen was caught in the Beaume river near its confluence with the Ardèche.

The habitat of the apron is fast-flowing, shallow rocky streams with a bottom of large boulders under which it can hide. It lives on the bottom, hiding under stones in the day and feeding mainly at night. In the Beaume it is accompanied by trout, chub, minnows, blageon, toxostome, Mediterranean barbel and common barbel.

Breeding and growth

The apron spawns from February to April laying its eggs in the shallows. The young fry live near the surface until they reach 2 cm (¾ in) long when they begin life among the stones on the bottom.

Feeding

The apron feeds on worms, insect larvae, small crustaceans and sometimes small fish and the ova of other species.

Fishing for apron

We heard no reports of the apron having been caught by fishermen. A small worm fished at night in deep places behind large stones would offer the best chance of catching it.

Characteristics

1st dorsal fin: 9–10 spines.
2nd dorsal fin: 10 rays.

Apron, river Baume. Photographed 16 May.

Apron. We couldn't resist a second picture of this great rarity.

Blageon from river Baume, Ardèche, France. Photographed 16 May.

Blageon

Blageon. *Leuciscus souffia* Risso. Family *Cyprinidae*. Italian, vairone; German, Stromer. Sometimes also called in French soufie or suiffe.

Recognition and related species

The blageon is a small dace-like fish characterized by a greeny-blue stripe along its side. This stripe disappears easily if the fish is in cloudy water or when the fish has been long out of water, but reappears as irregular blotching when the fish is preserved.

The blageon may be distinguished from the dace by its 45–48 scales along its lateral line (48–52 in dace) as well as by its dark stripe. Some other species of dace also have dark body stripes, notably the Croatian dace (*L. polylepis*) from northern Yugoslavia, and are even more similar to the blageon.

Three subspecies of blageon have been recognized in France, subspecies *agaz* in the Durance, Isère and Ardèche (illustrated here); subspecies *souffia* from the Var river which enters the sea at Nice and subspecies *mutelicus* from the Bevara river which flows into north-west Italy.

Habitat and distribution

The blageon is found from the Rhône basin north to the headwaters of the Rhine and eastwards to the Danube along the Alps, and in northern Italy in the Po basin. It favours small clear streams and lakes in the mountains where it may be found in shoals, with trout, minnow and Mediterranean barbel, and the shallower reaches of larger rivers where it is found in the company of other coarse fish. In some of these, hybrids are common between the blageon and the toxostome. From the fisheries standpoint the blageon is considered a nuisance as it breeds very quickly and competes with trout, at the same time never reaching a size to make it worth fishing for.

Breeding and growth

Blageon spawn in spring, laying their eggs over gravel in running water. They average around 10 cm (4 in), maximum size being 25 cm (10 in).

Feeding

Blageon feed on insect larvae, worms and small crustaceans, as well as on surface food such as small mayflies and sedges. Some algae may also be eaten.

Fishing for blageon

While not regarded as a useful sporting species because of its small size, the blageon is often fished for as it is a good bait for pike. Blageon take small worms or rise freely to a small black dry fly.

Characteristics

Dorsal fin: 8–9 branched rays.
Anal fin: 8–9 branched rays.
Pharyngeal teeth 4 (or 5) + 2.
Scales in the lateral line: 45–8.

River Ardèche, France.

Schneider *(not illustrated)*

Schneider. *Alburnoides bipunctatus* Block, Family *Cyprinidae*. French, spirlin; German, Schneider; Dutch, gestippelde alver.

Recognition and related species

The schneider is a small, bleak-like fish, but is usually deeper in the body, and has a dark stripe along its side. This is the best way to distinguish it from the bleak as otherwise the two species are very similar, both having a rather long-based anal fin. Schneider also differ from bleak in having less than 15 as opposed to 17–22 gill rakers, and a mouth which is not clearly superior, but has jaws of equal length.

In colour the schneider is mainly olive-green on the back with a darkish stripe along the side, and pale golden below. The ventral and anal fins are tinted orange at their base.

Habitat and distribution

Small streams are the usual habitat of the schneider, where it is often found in company with minnow and trout, much higher upriver than bleak. It prefers quiet places such as pools and the still water above weirs.

Schneider are not found in the British Isles, nor along the Atlantic coast of Europe, but from eastern France across central Europe to Russia and the Danube basin and as far as the Caspian and Aral seas.

Breeding and growth

Spawning takes place in summer, from May to July, over gravelly shallows.

Adult length of about 10 cm (4 in) is reached in four or five years. Exceptional specimens may measure 16 cm (6¼ in).

Feeding

Small insects and crustaceans form the major part of the diet of the schneider.

Characteristics

Dorsal fin: 7–8 rays.
Anal fin: 14–17 rays.
Scales along the lateral line: 44–52.
Pharyngeal teeth: 5 and 2 in two rows, or 4 and 2.

Toxostome from river Baume, Ardèche. Photographed 18 May.

Toxostome or French Nase

Toxostome. *Chondrostoma toxostoma* Val. Family *Cyprinidae*. French, nase or soiffe; Spanish, madrilla.

Recognition and related species
The toxostome is very similar to the nase but is usually smaller and where the two species occur in the same river, is found higher upstream. The anatomical differences between the toxostome and the nase are given on p.66. The toxostome is usually more green or olive on the flanks than the nase and has a slightly less protuberant snout and a more pointed lower jaw.
In rivers where the two are found together hybrids between blageon and toxostome are frequent. They are intermediate between the two species and do not have a dark stripe along the body.

Habitat and distribution
The toxostome is usually found in clear stony streams and the shallow parts of rivers in the foothills. It lives in small shoals in pools behind stones or rocks or in stiller places near the edge. It is restricted to western France and northern Spain and Portugal, from the Rhône and upper reaches of the Loire and Allier, westwards to the rivers which run down from the Pyrenees, and into central Portugal. An eastern Spanish stock is sometimes considered a distinct subspecies, subsp. *arrigonis*.

Breeding and growth
The toxostome spawns in shallow water over gravel after an upstream migration. Its usual spawning time is April, or when the water reaches 13°C (55°F).
Average size is about 20 cm (8 in) and a weight of 125 gm (4 oz). The maximum recorded length is 30 cm (12 in).

Feeding
The diet of toxostome is similar to that of the nase, consisting of algae attached to stones and other aquatic plants.

Fishing for toxostome
Because it lives in the same stretches of river that are suitable for trout, barbel and other fish that are more valuable or grow to a large size, the toxostome is not regularly fished for. Small pieces of bread flake would probably be the most likely bait.

Characteristics
Dorsal fin: 10 rays.
Anal fin: 8–9 rays.
Scales in the lateral line: 52–56.
Pharyngeal teeth: 6 in one row, compressed, knife-like.

River Ouvézè in flood.

River Test, Hampshire.

Dace

Dace. *Leuciscus leuciscus* Linn. Family *Cyprinidae*. French, vandoise; German, Hasel; Swedish, stäm; Dutch, serpeling.

Recognition and related species

The dace is similar to the chub, but of lighter build and generally smaller. The two are best distinguished by the shape of the anal and dorsal fins, concave on the edge in the dace, convex or straight in the chub; all the chub's fins appear more rounded, and it has a distinctly broader head. The orfe is also rather similar to the dace, but is usually deeper bodied and has more (56–61) scales along the lateral line. Dace are often confused with roach, but are most easily distinguished by the yellow, not red, eye and the slimmer body.

Habitat and distribution

Dace are usually found in clear, rather fast-flowing lowland streams and rivers, usually those with a gravelly bottom and often in company with trout. They also live in the faster stretches of slow rivers, in the same areas as chub, but lying in faster, shallower water. It has been noticed in some places that small dace prefer to live in slower water, and that larger ones migrate into areas of faster water, or to the upstream sections of short rivers. Dace tend to swim in shoals, lying just under the surface in summer, often in the shade of trees or bridges. They are also occasionally found in lakes.

In Britain, dace are found throughout England, but are less common in Wales, the west country and the north. They appear to be absent from Scotland, and in Ireland are found only in the Blackwater. On the Continent they have a more northerly distribution than the chub, being absent from Spain and Italy but extending eastwards across Siberia to the Arctic Ocean.

Breeding and growth

Dace spawn earlier than other related *Cyprinidae*, often in March and April, in shallow water among weed or stones. Because of this early spawning they are not likely to form hybrids with other species such as roach or chub. Though hybrids with bleak and rudd are mentioned by Newdyke (1979), their existence has not been confirmed. Adult length is about 15 cm (6 in) which is reached in four or five years. A one-year-old fish is usually about 6 cm (5¼ in) long. The maximum weight is 600 gm (1 lb 5 oz) and the British record is 574 gm (1¼ lb), caught by J. L. Gasson in the Little Ouse at Thetford.

Dace from river Kennet, Berkshire. Photographed 29 November.

Feeding
Dace eat insects, both larvae and adults, as well as crustaceans and some plants. In summer they tend to concentrate on floating food, and rise freely to small flies.

Fishing for dace
Dace may be caught on the same baits as are used for small roach or bleak, a maggot being the most convenient bait, though hemp seed is also recommended. They also rise freely to a small fly, but are often difficult to hook, requiring quick reactions and a fast strike. Suitable patterns are those used for trout, and a black gnat is a favourite. Wet-fly fishing into the runs can also be successful, the fly being similar to that used for chub, but smaller.

Characteristics
Dorsal fin: 8–9 rays.
Anal fin: 9–10 rays.
Scales along the lateral line: 48–51.
Pharyngeal teeth: 5 and 2–3 in two rows.

Immature dace from river Wey.

River Baume, Ardèche, France.

Mediterranean barbel

Mediterranean barbel. *Barbus meridionalis* Risso. Family *Cyprinidae*.
French, barbeau truite, barbeau méridionale, durgan; Italian, barbo
canio.

Recognition and related species

The Mediterranean barbel is easily distinguished from the common
barbel by the irregular dark spots and blotches on its head and back
though these vary in intensity according to the type of bottom on which
the fish was living. It is also generally smaller, and lacks the serrations on
the longest ray of the dorsal fin.

Other species of barbel are spotted, notably *Barbus prespensis* from
northern Greece, but none have the large spots characteristic of
B. meridionalis.

Small specimens resemble gudgeon, which are sometimes found in the
same streams, but the gudgeon has only two barbels, not four as have all
the barbels.

Habitat and distribution

The Mediterranean barbel is found in the southern foothills of the Alps,
the Massif Centrale and the Pyrenees, and also in Greece and in the
Danube basin. Several subspecies have been named, representing
populations that have been isolated from each other since a warmer
interglacial period.

In France it is especially common in the Rhône tributaries south of
Lyon, and it is also found in the Var and Argens.

It usually lives in small rivers and side streams at around 500 m
(1,640 ft), particularly where they run in gorges, lying in deep pools
below waterfalls and under rock ledges. Many of these streams are
spring-fed and some water remains in them even in long periods of

drought. In others the stream below the zone where the barbel live may
even become dry. In such streams it is accompanied by trout, minnow
and blageon.

Breeding and growth

Spawning takes place from May to July, usually after an upstream
migration in shallow running water over gravel.

Adult size is 20–30 cm (8–12 in), with a maximum of 40 cm (16 in).
A 25 cm (10 in) specimen weighs about 250 gm (8 oz).

Feeding

Habits and diet are similar to the common barbel; the Mediterranean
barbel lives on the bottom and feeds on crustaceans, insect larvae,
worms, etc.

Fishing for Mediterranean barbel

The Mediterranean barbel is not particularly popular with anglers, but
can be caught on small worms or cheese allowed to drift into likely holes
or under ledges.

Cooking Mediterranean barbel

Mediterranean barbel are said to be good to eat, small specimens treated
like gudgeon, which they somewhat resemble, larger ones like trout. We
did not taste the ones we caught, but they were plump, and coming from
clean water would probably have had good flavour.

Characteristics

Dorsal fin: 9 rays.
Anal fin: 6 rays.
Scales along the lateral line: 48–55.
Pharyngeal teeth: 5, 3, and 2 in three rows.

Mediterranean barbel from tiny tributary of Ardèche, with soapwort flowers.

River Loddon, Hampshire.

Barbel

Barbel. *Barbus barbus* Linn. Family *Cyprinidae*. French, barbeau fluviatile; German, Barbe; Dutch, barbeel.

Recognition and related species

The barbel is a fine fish, easily recognized by its streamlined body with golden scales, and its elongated snout with four barbels, two small by the tip of the nose and two longer by the back of the mouth. Its dorsal fin is few-rayed, strongly concave, and pointed, as is the upper fork of the tail. The gudgeon, which is a similar overall shape, is usually much smaller, has only two barbels and its back and fins have brownish markings. There are many other species of *Barbus* in eastern and southern Europe. The Mediterranean barbel (see p.62) is a generally smaller fish with a spotted back. Another species, *B. comiza*, is found in southern Spain, and there are other rare species in small areas in Greece, Albania, Turkey and in the Black and Caspian seas.

Habitat and distribution

The barbel is a bottom-living fish, inhabiting relatively fast-flowing stretches in the middle reaches of large rivers, such as the Thames, or deeper pools in smaller rivers. They like to lie near weirs or in holes behind tree roots or fallen logs, rock ledges or other obstructions on the river bed, especially in places where the bottom is gravelly.

On the Continent the barbel is found from France eastwards to the Danube basin and across Germany and Poland to western Russia. In the British Isles the barbel was formerly confined to southward and eastward flowing rivers such as the Dorset Stour, Hampshire Avon, Trent, the Yorkshire Ouse, the Thames and their tributaries, but it has now been introduced into the Severn where it has proved successful and become well established. It is not known in Ireland or Scotland.

Breeding and growth

Barbel spawn from May to July, moving upstream before laying their eggs among gravel and stones in running water. The female makes a redd, rather similar to that of a salmon; the males develop tubercles along their head and back.

The adult length of 25–75 cm (10–30 in) is reached in four or five years, and a 50 cm (20 in) fish weighs about 2.3 kg (5 lb). The maximum size is about 90 cm (3 ft) and a weight of 7.25 kg (16 lb): the British record was a fish of 7.525 kg (16 lb 1 oz) from the Hampshire Avon, foul-hooked while fishing for salmon, and many other specimens over 6 and 6.5 kg (13 and 14 lb) have been caught.

Feeding

Barbel feed almost exclusively on the bottom, and will eat almost anything: worms, molluscs, crustacean and insect larvae as well as vegetable matter and, when larger, small fish. Sir Herbert Maxwell, writing at the beginning of the century said, 'barbel . . . . rejoice in the most filthy substances discharged in sewage; wherefore the activity of the Thames conservancy board and the county councils in purifying the Thames must have deprived barbel of some of their favourite comestibles'.

Fishing for barbel

Because of its large size, great strength and stamina, and its liking for fast water the barbel is a popular sporting fish. It fights well when hooked, and does not give up until completely exhausted. For this reason is should be unhooked promptly, returned to the water as quickly as possible, and if necessary held gently on an even keel until it has regained the energy to swim away. This may take some minutes if the fish has been out of water too long. Liberal groundbaiting is recommended for the preparation of a good barbel swim, both in advance, and while fishing. In the past, lob worms were thrown in in great numbers, either loose in slow places or encased in a ball of clay mixed with bran, so they were slowly released into the swim and not swept away in fast water. Now a swim-feeder is used, which can release a stream of bait into exactly the right place.

Barbel normally feed on the bottom, so a ledger is used to keep the bait near the fish.

For fishing longer swims a large float can be tried, and the bait allowed to move along the bottom. Worms were the traditional hookbait, but luncheon meat is now favoured, cut into ¼ in cubes. Bread flake, cheese or maggots are also suitable baits.

The official British rod-caught record is 6.24 kg (13 lb 12 oz), caught by J. Day on the Royalty Fishery on the Hampshire Avon in 1962.

Cooking barbel

Although caught commercially in large numbers in eastern Europe, the barbel has never been considered a good food fish in England. Its flesh is said to be insipid, and its roe is reputed to be poisonous; we have not been tempted to test this reputation!

Characteristics

Dorsal fin: about 3 bony and 8 soft rays; one bony ray modified into a serrated spine.
Anal fin: about 3 bony and 8 soft rays.
Scales in the lateral line: 55–65.
Pharyngeal teeth: 5, 3 and 2 in three rows.

Barbel from river Loddon. Photographed 6 October.

Gorges of the Ardèche, France.

Nase

Nase. *Chondrostoma nasus* Linn. Family *Cyrinidae*. French, hotu, nase, musard; German, Nase, Näsling; Dutch, sneep.

Recognition and related species

The nase is a slender-bodied silvery fish with reddish fins. Its characteristic feature is its mouth and snout. The snout is protuberant and rounded, the mouth is small, beneath the snout and has horny lips. Two other related fish have similar protuberant snouts; the Vimba (p.124), a species which lives in the lower reaches of rivers, and has a much longer based anal fin, and the toxostome or French nase. The nase is usually larger than the toxostome and found lower down the same rivers. The differences between the two are small; the nase has 10–12 rays in the anal fin (8–9 in the toxostome), and 59–62 scales in the lateral line (52–56 in the toxostome).

Other species of nase (*Chondrostoma*) are found in the Po in north Italy (*C. soetta* and *C. genei*), Portugal and west Spain (*C. polylepis*), Yugoslavia (*C. kneri* and *C. phoxinus*) and in the Caucasian rivers (*C. oxyrhynchum* and *C. colchicum*).

Hybrids are common between the nase and the toxostome where the two are found in the same stretch of river, and are also recorded between the nase and the chub.

Habitat and distribution

The nase is found in fast, rather shallow, water in the middle reaches of large rivers and often congregates behind the piles of bridges or in rough water caused by rocky ledges or banks of gravel. It is gregarious and swims in shoals of individuals of a single age. At present the nase is found between western France and western Russia, south to the Balkans and Turkey and north to the hilly parts of central Germany and the hills near Moscow. There is some evidence that it is native only in northern France, and that it has spread through the canal system into the Massif Centrale and the Rhône, where it is now common. Its original distribution would thus have complemented that of the toxostome which was found in the Rhône and Loire basins and in northern Spain.

Breeding and growth

Nase spawn in shallow gravelly areas and in tributaries, after an upstream migration, often congregating in large shoals. The usual time is between February and April when the water temperature reaches 11°C (52°F). The sticky eggs adhere to the stones.

Nase are usually around 30 cm (1 ft) long, but specimens up to 50 cm (20 in) and weighing almost 1.8 kg (4 lb) are recorded.

Feeding

The nase feeds primarily on algae which grow on the rocky and stony bottoms of the rivers in which it lives and its thick lips are adapted to scrape the algae off the stones.

Fishing for nase

Because of their specialized diet, nase are not often taken by anglers, but some, and especially the larger specimens, have been caught – probably since they are less exclusively algae eaters. In the large rivers of eastern Europe the nase is caught commercially in large numbers. We have had no experience of cooking or eating nase, but a Frenchman offered some of those we caught on the Ardèche declined them with a sniff!

Characteristics

Dorsal fin: 12 rays.
Anal fin: 10–12 rays.
Scales in the lateral line: 57–62.
Pharyngeal teeth: 6.

Nase from river Ardèche. Note the big nose. Photographed 16 May.

River Wey, Surrey.

Chub

Chub. *Leuciscus cephalus* Linn. Family *Cyprinidae*. French, chevaine; German, Döbel; Swedish, färna; Dutch, meun. Old English names, chevin, loggerhead, skelly (Cumberland).

Recognition and related species

The chub is one of the larger of the carp family and one of the more slender-bodied. Its fins are rich red, rounded, and have relatively few rays. Its scales are large and its wide mouth has no barbels. It can be distinguished from the dace by its convex or straight anal and dorsal fins, its redder fins and wider mouth, and from the roach by its fewer (7–9) rayed anal fin and more slender body. The orfe is also very similar to the chub, but it has 56–61 scales along the lateral line, and a concave anal fin.

Hybrids involving chub are not common, but ones with bleak, roach and rudd have been confirmed.

Habitat and distribution

Chub are characteristic of rivers with a moderate flow, for example the Thames or slower stretches of the Wye or the Severn. They tend to inhabit the same areas as barbel, the barbel living on the bottom, the chub swimming higher in the water. They are occasionally also found in lakes and a population is said to be established in Lake Vyrnwy in Wales. In summer chub tend to lie in shoals close to the surface, often in shallow or streamy water where they can be seen basking, their fins appearing quite black. In winter they go for the deepest possible places in the river, and these chub holes are well known to local fishermen.

Chub are found throughout lowland England, but are rare in the West Country and in upland Wales, and not known in Scotland or Ireland. On the Continent they are found from France and Spain north to the Baltic and east to the Urals, the Caspian and throughout Turkey, where large shoals can be seen in the headwaters of the Euphrates.

Breeding and growth

Chub spawn in early summer, from April to June in England; the eggs are laid in shallow slow-flowing water, usually attached to plants or stones. Successful spawning is often irregular and many populations are dominated by individuals of one age. Their adult length is 30–45 cm (12–18 in), with a maximum of 80 cm (32 in). Specimens up to 7.5 kg (16 lb) are recorded on the Continent; the British record is 3.345 kg (7 lb 6 oz) caught on the Royalty Fishery, Hampshire, Avon in 1957 by W. L. Warren. Chub grow slowly and reach 10–15 cm (4–6 in) after two to three years. A 3.5 kg (8 lb) specimen is probably about twelve years old, though 1–1.5 kg (2–3 lb) is a more usual weight.

Feeding

When young, chub feed on insects, both larvae and adults, and crustaceans. When large they become predatory, eating small fish and frogs, and they are said even to take voles.

Fishing for chub

The chub is a popular sporting fish, and will take almost any bait, so long as it is not alarmed. Large worms are successful, but bread paste, cheese or luncheon meat are popular baits. In summer many chub are caught on artificial flies, both dry and wet, often by fishermen after trout or salmon. Suitable flies are anything with silver and red in them, imitating a small fish, and rather larger than would be used for trout. Spinning with a small spoon is also likely to be successful.

In winter, when the chub are near the bottom, ledgering is most likely to be effective, as the deep holes in which the fish lie have to be explored with the bait.

Chub are universally considered useless as food, the flesh being soft and full of sharp bones.

Characteristics

Dorsal fin: 9–10 rays.
Anal fin: 8–10 rays.
Scales along the lateral line: 44–46.
Pharyngeal teeth: 5 large and 2 smaller in two rows.

Pike

Pike. *Esox lucius* Linn. Family *Esocidae*. French, brochet; German, Hecht; Swedish, gädda; Dutch, snoek; Finnish, hauki.

Recognition and related species
The pike is the most purely predatory fish in European waters, and its long jaws full of sharp teeth make it instantly recognizable. The body is elongated, brown and green mottled for camouflage and its single dorsal fin is set well back towards the tail. There are no other species of pike in Europe, but there are several in North America, including the mighty Muskellunge, *E. masquinongy* which may weigh over 450 kg (100 lb). A smaller species, *E. reicherti*, is found in eastern Siberia, in the Amur river.

Habitat and distribution
Pike are found in all waters which are not too fast-flowing, from large clear lakes such as Lough Corrib and Loch Lomond, to canals and ponds, and to chalk streams and muddy rivers in lowland England. Except while spawning they tend to live solitary lives, often in or near reed beds or in shallower water, waiting to ambush passing fish, and large specimens are found particularly at the junctions of tributaries with the main river. In lakes, they may be in open water; in Windermere, for instance, the pike follow the shoals of char on to the spawning beds, and in Loch Lomond they have been observed following and harrying shoals of powan, in the same way that lions follow migrating herds of wildebeest.

Pike are found throughout the northern hemisphere, both in Eurasia and in America. In North America they are called northern pike and are common all through Canada with the exception of the far north, into Alaska and the northern United States, roughly north of a line from Pennsylvania to Nebraska. In Eurasia, pike are found from Ireland and the Baltic catchment area, south to the Pyrenees and northern Turkey and across Siberia to the Pacific Ocean north of Kamchatka.

Breeding and growth
Pike spawn in spring, between March and May, though the adults are usually paired and on the spawning grounds by February or March. Spawning usually occurs in shallow water, in small streams, lagoons off the main river or sheltered bays in lakes or even in ditches. The eggs are laid on weeds; water-crowfoot is a favourite, but any small-leaved weed in the right place is used, such as *Elodea* (Canadian pondweed), *Myriophyllum* (water milfoil), or the dead remains of sedges.

The male pike arrive first on the spawning grounds, the females some days later, and more than one male may pair with each female. The males are generally smaller, and male pike greater than 4.5 kg (10 lb) weight are distinctly rare. Buller (1979) says that less than one in a hundred pike of 4.5 kg (10 lb) are male. He advances an interesting theory for this. During the act of spawning the male and female fish swim slowly forward, eye to eye, the female laying the eggs, the male fertilizing them. If the male was equal in length to the female the milt cloud would be released behind the falling eggs (especially if the spawning was taking place in a current), which would fail to be fertilized. If the male is smaller the milt will have time to pass through the egg masses as they are laid, and so fertilization can take place. Natural selection would thus favour smaller males which could fertilize eggs from a larger number of females. Large males would be at an advantage only if they were preferred by large females which produce more eggs.

In contrast with some other species, e.g. chub, the recruitment of pike fry is fairly regular from year to year, so pike of a variety of sizes are usually found in one area. Young pike grow quickly, and at three weeks old are actively carnivorous and both capable of eating, and inclined to eat, their own siblings. Actual growth rates vary greatly depending on the supply of food. A typical example is 25 cm (10 in) after one year, 6.8–7.6 cm (17–19 in) after two years; 4 kg (9 lb) and 9.2–12.4 cm (23–31 in) after four years; thereafter weight and length increase depend even more on food supply. In one sample of large Irish pike, eight-year-old fish ranged from 10.5–22.5 kg (23–50 lb), and in Windermere 13.5 kg (30 lb) fish varied from eleven to eighteen years old.

The maximum weight for a pike is probably in the region of 34 kg (75 lb), and pike of this size are indicated from Russia by Alwyne Wheeler. Fred Buller, in his fascinating book *The Pike*, has carefully noted all the large pike recorded in the British Isles. He reckons that the largest was probably the Endrick Pike, which was found dead in about 1934 near the River Endrick, a tributary of Loch Lomond; the length of its head suggests that it weighed about 31.5 kg (70 lb) when it was in its prime. A similarly huge fish is recorded as being captured by John Murray, the keeper at Kemore in Galloway, in Loch Ken, some time

Jack pike, from Cowley Lake. Photographed 18 December.

Cowley Lake, Middlesex.

Inlet of the Baltic near Parainen, Finland.

around 1774. It is supposed to have weighed 33 kg (72 lb), and a weight of between 27 and 31.5 kg (60–70 lb) was confirmed by Tate Regan when he measured the skull in about 1911.

The largest caught on a rod and line was a 24 kg (53 lb) fish taken by John Garvin in Lough Conn in 1920, on a brown and gold Devon. It is supposed to have regurgitated a 4.5 kg (10 lb) salmon when it was landed. Its head is preserved in the British Museum (Natural History). More recent and less romantic monsters have been netted from Lough Mask by the Inland Fisheries Trust. 23 kg (50½ lb), 22 kg (48 lb), 20.5 kg (46 lb), and 20 kg (45 lb) fish were caught between 1957 and 1966. These four were female fish netted as they came into the spawning grounds, and show that 24 kg (53 lb) is a perfectly likely weight for John Garvin's fish.

Feeding

From a very early age, young pike are carnivorous, living primarily on other small fish. Larger ones will take any other animal or bird that they can get, and ducks and rats are regularly eaten.

It is interesting to note that most of the really huge pike come from waters with a good run of salmon, or a big stock of large trout or other fish. Lough Conn is well stocked with salmon from the River Moy, and Loch Ken from the Kirkcudbright Dee; the Endrick Pike certainly came up from Loch Lomond. To grow to 22.5 kg (50 lb) a pike needs a really good supply of food of large size since pike prefer a prey of 10–25% of their own body weight; for example a 3.75 kg (8½ lb) salmon was found in one 14 kg (32 lb) pike taken from Lough Conn.

The total weight of fish a pike must consume in a year has been found to be less than might be expected: to maintain its body weight a pike needs a yearly intake of 1.4 times its own weight; to put on 500 gm (1 lb) in weight a pike must eat approximately 2.5 kg (5 lb) of fish.

This means that a 9 kg (20 lb) pike which grows to 11.5 kg (25 lb) at the end of the year, must eat about 24 kg (53 lb) of fish in that year.

Fishing for pike

The pike is very popular among those anglers who like to fish for it, but regarded with either suspicion or hate by the rest.

Pike are regularly caught on live baits, dead baits, plugs or spoons, imitations of birds and rats, and even, particularly in America, on special flies.

Pike fishing is usually done in cold weather during the winter, and it is then that big pike are at their maximum weight, but their period of greatest food requirement is late June, so that is when they should be hungriest.

Anyone interested in large pike or in pike fishing is recommended to read *The Pike* by Fred Buller who goes into both the giant specimens, and techniques for catching them, in great detail.

The official British rod-caught record is 18.14 kg (40 lb), caught by P. D. Hancock from Horsey Mere, Norfolk in 1967.

Cooking pike

When considered as food, few fish are the subject of such conflicting views and reports as the pike.

The most famous use for it is to convert it into quenelles and eat it with some suitably delicious sauce. Elizabeth David describes the 'tedious and lengthy' business of making perfect quenelles, 'involving much pounding and sieving of the flesh of the pike, blending it with a *panade*, cream, white of egg, etc.', and warns the unwary against stodgy mass-produced alternatives (though with care, good quenelles can be made in a food processor). An appropriate sauce is a *beurre blanc*, and this can also be used to complement a pike baked whole. Fred Buller's recommendations for filleting the pike, cooking the fillets, and making fish cakes with them is more suitable for the English palate. The quality of the pike's flesh is likely to depend on two factors: the condition of the fish and the water from which it came, and hence its diet. A pike from a deep, clean loch grown fat on a diet of salmon or trout will taste better than one from a muddy river which has existed on roach and bream. I think that pike is best cooked simply, by baking in foil and serving with butter and lemon. A nice pike served this way is superb.

Characteristics

Dorsal fin: 19 rays. Anal fin: 19 rays.

Pike from river Loddon, with giant Butterbur leaves. Photographed 6 October.

A small lake near Ruovesi, Finland.

Perch

Perch. *Perca fluviatilis* Linn. Family *Percidae*. French, perche; German, Barsch; Dutch, baars; Swiss, Egli. East Anglia and Lincolnshire, barse.

Recognition and related species

The perch is easily recognized by its deep body marked with about five dark vertical bars, its spiny forward or first dorsal fin and smaller non-spiny second dorsal fin, and by its red ventral and anal fins and tail. The most similar species are the zander (p.76), which has similar but pale fins, a longer body and a forward dorsal fin which is the same length or shorter than the second; and the ruffe (p.78) which is always much smaller and pale brownish in colour, lacking the black bars and red fins; its two dorsal fins are joined. Two other fish which may be encountered in Britain have two separate dorsal fins; the largemouth bass (p.114), a native of North America, has the second dorsal fin larger than the first, and two spiny rays in its ventral fin.

Habitat and distribution

Perch are common in still water and slow-flowing rivers throughout the British Isles and western Europe. They are rare in Scotland and other mountainous areas and they avoid really poor acid lakes and rocky rivers. They are especially numerous in recently-flooded reservoirs and gravel pits, possibly because their ribbons of eggs can be spread by waterbirds, and they can quickly colonize these new waters. They also form an important part of the fish population in large clear lakes such as Windermere and others in the Lake District, Loch Lomond, Lough Corrib and other Irish limestone loughs, and the Norfolk Broads. Shoals of smaller perch can often be seen in clear sandy bays, darting away as the boat glides in; the larger ones often frequent piers or landing stages, and can be seen lurking near the piles, or met unexpectedly eye to eye while diving!
In rivers, perch prefer clearer, cleaner water, either in streamy stretches where trout, dace and chub are common, or in deeper slower places among roach and pike.

Breeding and growth

Perch spawn in spring, between March and June. The eggs are white, 2.3 mm (¹⁄₁₀ in) in diameter, and are laid in mucus in long ribbons or masses on waterweeds, dead twigs or any other obstruction. Indeed one method of controlling them is to lay bundles of branches in the water, and remove them once they are covered with eggs. Perch are also trapped most easily in spring, when they will congregate around and in wirenetting traps placed in about ten feet of water.
The fry spend the summer months in large shoals in shallow water, where they may often be seen skittering on the surface, pursued by a wave made by some larger perch, trout or pike.

The average size of adult perch in Britain is from 15 to 30 cm (6–12 in), and a 1 kg (2 lb) fish is a very good one. Specimens up to 3 kg (7 lb) have been reported from English waters in the past, but the present acknowledged record stands at 2.23 kg (4 lb 14 oz), caught by Mrs E. N. Owen in Kings Lake, Romsey, in March 1984. The Irish record, from Lough Erne is 2.75 kg (5 lb 8 oz). On the Continent perch run larger, up to 6.5 kg (14 lb).
Even when adult, perch tend to swim in shoals of one age group. The numbers in a shoal decrease sharply each year, until the largest are solitary, or are found in twos or threes.
In the 1960s and '70s perch ulcer disease spread throughout England, killing most of the perch, especially the large ones. For example, the Freshwater Biological Association at Windermere estimated that 99% of the perch in that lake were killed by the disease in 1976.

Feeding

Perch are almost entirely carnivorous, eating larvae of aquatic insects, worms, shrimps and any small fish, but especially their own fry.

Fishing for perch

Small perch are easy to catch on maggots, worms or artificial flies and lures, especially bright silver-bodied patterns which imitate small fish. They have, however, a particular reputation for inexplicably refusing to bite on some days.
The larger the perch, the more wary he is, and the more difficult to catch. Large lob worms are a good bait for them, or small live bait – a roach or gudgeon – or a dead bait fished on the bottom. In summer the larger specimens are likely to be found in deep places near stands of reeds or bullrushes, or in clearings in a weed bed, all places from which they can ambush their prey. The angler should be mobile, moving cautiously upriver, casting into likely places. Perch continue to feed in cold weather, and even large specimens will congregate in winter in deep holes.

Cooking perch

Perch are excellent to eat and unjustly neglected in England. In Switzerland, where good specimens used to abound in most of the large lakes, Eglifilet is a great speciality, as good as fillet of sole. I have found smaller specimens delicious when cooked in a small smoker: if very fresh, they need not be cleaned, and after smoking the skin hardens and peels off easily, and the firm white flesh separates cleanly from the bones.

Characteristics

1st dorsal fin: 14–15 spines. 2nd dorsal fin: 1–2 spines, 13–14 rays. Ventral fin: 1 spine, 5 rays. Anal fin: 2 spines, 8–9 rays. Scales in the lateral line: 50–70.

Perch from Darwell Reservoir, Sussex. Photographed 6 October.

Sixteen foot drain, Cambridgeshire.

Zander

Zander or pike-perch. *Stizostedion lucioperca* Linn. Family *Percidae*. French, sandre; German, Zander; Swedish, gös; Dutch, snoekbaars; Finnish, kuka.

Recognition and related species

The zander can be recognized by its two perch-like dorsal fins, and its slender body with a long head, large eyes and jaws armed with sharp teeth. It can be distinguished from the perch by having its second dorsal fin larger than the first (front) dorsal, and by its paler, not bright red fins. From the ruffe, also closely related, the zander can be distinguished by its more slender body, and by having the two dorsal fins separate, not united into a single fin. Ruffe are also much smaller fish, but can be confused with young zander. The sea bass is also rather zander-like but it has only 8–9 rather than 11–16 spiny rays in its first dorsal fin. A related species of zander, *Stizostedion volgensis* is found in the Volga, the Danube and rivers in between. It differs in having 9–10 rays in the anal fin, and 70–83 scales in the lateral line.

Habitat and distribution

The zander is usually found in lakes, canals, and slow-flowing rivers. It prefers rather cloudy, open water, and usually feeds at night or in the daytime only when the water is especially muddy.

Zander are native to eastern Europe and western Asia, but have been introduced into the Rhine area, much of France and eastern England. The original introduction to England was made by the ninth Duke of Bedford in 1878. He introduced twenty-three zander from Schleswig-Holstein into two lakes in Woburn Park, the Shoulder of Mutton pond, and the Basin Lake. A second introduction was made by the eleventh Duke in about 1910. The zander did not spread significantly until 1963 when ninety-seven 15–25 cm (6–10 in) fish were put into the Great Ouse Relief Channel by Norman McKenzie, head of the Great Ouse River Authority. From here they spread very quickly through the canals and rivers of East Anglia, and are now established in the Cam and the Lark, as well as the Great Ouse itself. Recently they have been reported from the Nene.

Breeding and growth

Zander spawn in shallow water from April to June. Their eggs are laid over sand or shingle, or among the roots of reeds. Young fish swim in shoals, while the largest ones are solitary.

The maximum size reached by zander on the Continent is about 130 cm (50 in) and 12 kg (26½ lb). The largest caught in England is 7.824 kg (17 lb 4 oz) from the Great Ouse Relief Channel in 1977, by D. Litton.

Feeding

Zander are primarily predatory and take small fish of all kinds, but particularly bream, roach, and ruffe, as these are commonest in most of the waters where zander are found.

In the rivers in the Fenland, zander are alleged to have caused a massive reduction in the stocks of Cyprinids (carp family), following their introduction and population explosion.

In other waters, however, e.g. Claydon Water in Buckinghamshire, they live in reasonable balance with large numbers of carp, with bream, roach and gudgeon, as well as catfish.

In Finland they are common in lowland acid lakes with ruffe and perch, on which they feed, burbot and many *Cyprinidae*.

Fishing for zander

Being active predators, zander are fished for with live bait or dead bait, on tackle similar to but more delicate than that used for pike. Wire traces are not needed, and the line may be around 4 kg (9 lb) breaking strain. The most successful bait fishes are ruffe, gudgeon, bleak, small perch or bream, though sprats or small herrings may also be used, as they are for pike. Zander are said to take best in the evening or at night, in dull weather, or when the water is coloured. When a zander is caught which is not required for eating, it should be returned to the water immediately and handled with care, as damaged fish easily become infected with fungus. Some angling associations now insist that all zander caught are killed, because of the great reduction they've caused in the smaller cyprinids.

Cooking zander

In countries where they are common, such as Finland, zander are popular for eating. The flesh is very good, white, flaky and not oily; it is similar to that of its relative, the perch, and is prepared in the same way.

Characteristics

1st dorsal fin: 13–14 spines. 2nd dorsal fin: 2 spines and 17–19 rays. Anal fin: 2–3 spines, 11–13 rays. Scales along the lateral line: 80–95.

Zander from fen drain in Cambridgeshire, living in muddy water. Photographed 10 October.

Zander, Lake Jäminginselkä, Finland, living in clear peaty water. Photographed 27 June.

Ruffe from river Colne, Middlesex. Photographed 17 July.

Ruffe

Ruffe or pope. *Gymnocephalus cernuus* Linn. Family *Percidae*. French, gremille; German, Kaulbarsh; Swedish, gars; Dutch, pos; Finnish, kiiski.

Recognition and related species

The ruffe is like a small, mottled, sand-coloured perch, seldom more than 15 cm (6 in) long. It has the same rather deep-shouldered body shape as the perch, but its two dorsal fins are not separate but run into one another. The zander, which is less clearly barred than the perch, also has distinctly separate dorsal fins, but has a slenderer body. Other ruffe-like fish are found in eastern Europe. *Gymnocephalus acerina* is found in the Don and other rivers flowing into the north of the Black Sea; it differs in its longer snout, dorsal fin with more (17–19) spines, and in having more scales along the lateral line (50–55). A second species *G. schraetser* is found in the Danube; it also has a long head, more fin spines and scales, and three narrow stripes along each side.

Habitat and distribution

In England, ruffe are characteristic of slow rivers, canals and dykes in the south and east, but they are also found in some lakes, and have spread as far west as Lake Bala in north Wales and Loch Lomond. They are rare in south Wales, southwest England and Scotland, and absent from Ireland.
On the Continent they are found in western France, but have probably spread there through the canals, and are native only from the Rhine eastwards. Their southern limit appears to be the Alps and the Danube, and they extend eastwards across central Asia and northern Siberia. Ruffe are found in brackish water in the Baltic, and are common in Finland in acid lakes in company with zander, perch and burbot.

Breeding and growth

Ruffe spawn in spring, from March to May, laying their sticky eggs on weed or stones in shallow water. Initial growth of the fry is quite fast, but maturity is reached at two years and little growth takes place after that. Few live more than five years.
Average size is 10–15 cm (4–6 in), but specimens 45 cm (18 in) with a weight of about 750 gm (1½ lb) are recorded on the Continent.
The British rod-caught record is 148 gm (5 oz 4 drm) caught by R. J. Jenkins at West View Farm, Cumbria.

Feeding

Ruffe are mainly bottom feeders and insect larvae, especially bloodworms, and small crustacea make up most of their diet. Small fish and fish eggs may also be eaten.

Fishing for ruffe

A small worm or single maggot fished on the bottom is a good bait for ruffe, and once a shoal has found the bait many can usually be caught in one place. They are so small, however, that few bother to fish for them, and they are usually a curse to the angler after something better. Isaak Walton remarked that, 'no fish that swims is of a pleasanter taste', but we have not tested his assertion. They might be expected to taste like small perch, which are very good, with firm white flesh.

Characteristics

1st dorsal fin: 11–16 spines. 2nd dorsal fin: 11–15 rays.
Anal fin: 2 spines and 5–6 rays.
Scales in the lateral line: 35–40.

Bleak

Bleak. *Alburnus alburnus* Linn. Family *Cyprinidae*. French, ablette; German, Ukelei; Swedish, loja; Dutch, alver; Finnish, salakka.

Recognition and related species

Bleak are recognized by their slender silver bodies and steel blue or greenish back. Their mouth is characteristic, the lower lip protruding below the upper. They may be distinguished from small roach and dace also by their larger anal fin which has 20–23 rays, as opposed to 10–11 in the dace and 12–14 in the roach. From the breams which have rather similar fins, bleak are distinguished by their slender bodies.
Hybrids between chub and bleak, dace and bleak, and roach and bleak are all known, the first being the commonest, the other two rare.

Habitat and distribution

The bleak is a small and lively fish, found in rivers and more rarely in lakes. It is commonest in the middle reaches of the larger river systems of southern England, notably the Thames and its tributaries, the Medway, the Bristol Avon, the Severn, the Trent, the Humber rivers and the East Anglian Ouse. It appears to be absent from Ireland, Scotland, most of Wales, and England north and west of the Humber system. On the Continent bleak occur throughout Europe north of the Alps and Pyrenees, and eastwards to the Bosphorus and the river Volga.
Bleak are usually found in stretches with a smooth but steady flow, usually in the company of roach, dace and chub, though they may also be associated with bream and ruffe. On summer days they lie just under the surface, taking gnats, mosquitoes and other surface flies. In colder weather they lie in mid-water.

Breeding and growth

Bleak spawn from April to June, depositing their yellow eggs, 1.5 mm (¹/₁₆ in) in diameter, on to stones and other surfaces in running and still water. Adult length, 10–15 cm (4–6 in), is reached in about four years. The maximum recorded length is 25 cm (10 in). Bleak seldom weigh more than a few grams, the official British rod-caught record being 120 gm (4 oz 4 drm), caught in the river Monnow, Monmouth in 1982 by B. Derrington. Any outsize specimens are likely to be hybrids, probably with chub.

Feeding

Small insects, both larvae and adults, and crustacea are the regular food of bleak. Sir Herbert Maxwell records that they once grew fat on raw sewage effluent in the Thames, though whether directly on the sewage, or on the invertebrates associated with it, is not clear.

Fishing for bleak

Bleak are seldom specifically sought by the angler, though they may at times make a valuable contribution to the catch of the match fisherman when other larger species are not feeding. A single maggot or caster or a fat green caterpillar may catch them well, but they move very quickly and the angler must be alert and his strike immediate. A floating fly, either a natural bluebottle or a small artificial, may also be effective if the fish are seen feeding on the surface. Again delicate tackle and quick reactions are necessary for success.

Bleak are of little use for food, but were popular as bait, especially for large Thames trout. In the past, bleak scales were much used in the manufacture of simulated pearls. A silvery substance, guanin, extracted from the scales, was deposited on the inside of tiny glass balls which were made slightly irregular, and cunningly dulled on the surface, to look more natural.

Characteristics

Dorsal fin: 10–11 rays. Anal fin: 18–23 rays.
Scales in the lateral line: 55.
Less than 5 scales between anal fin and lateral line.
Pharyngeal teeth: 5 and 2 in two rows.

Backwater of river Thames at Hurley, Berkshire.

Belica (*not illustrated*)

Belica. *Leucaspius deliniatus* Heckel. Family *Cyprinidae*. French, able de Heckel; German, Moderlieschen; Swedish, groplöja; Dutch, vetje; Slovenian, belica.

Recognition and related species

The belica resembles a small delicate bleak but differs in its incomplete lateral line which ends forward of the dorsal fin, extending only for 8–10 scales. The anal fin has 10–13 rays, about 6 fewer than those of the bleak (p.78). In colour the belica is bright bluish-silver, with a dark greenish back.

Other species of *Leucaspius* are found in southern Europe, *L. marathonicus* around Marathon, and *L. stymphalicus* in the Peloponnese. A third species, *L. irideus* is confined to western Turkey, in the area around Bursa.

Habitat and distribution

Ponds, lakes and very slow stretches of rivers are the usual habitat of the belica.

It occurs from the Rhine basin eastwards to the Volga, Danube and Caucasian rivers, northwards to the southern Baltic.

Breeding and growth

In summer the female develops a small tube at the anus, by which the eggs are looped around water weeds (compare with bitterling p.110). June and July is the usual spawning season.

The young fish mature after two years, and rarely live more than five. Average size is 6–8 cm (2½–3 in) with a maximum of 12 cm (5 in).

Feeding

Both small aquatic invertebrates and delicate plants are eaten. Belica are said to be caught in nets in parts of Russia, but are too small to be of significance to anglers.

Bleak from river Wey. Photographed 13 November.

Characteristics

Dorsal fin: 8–9 rays. Anal fin: 10–13 rays.
Scales in the lateral line: line extends for 2–13 scales only.
Pharyngeal teeth: not recorded.

An inlet of the Baltic near Pargas, Finland.

Asp

Asp. *Aspius aspius* Linn. Family *Cyprinidae*. German, Rapjen; Swedish, asp; Finnish, toutain.

Recognition and related species
The asp is one of the few members of the carp family which has become almost exclusively fish-eating, and for this reason has evolved a large mouth and streamlined body. It is somewhat similar to a very large dace but has more pointed and more strongly concave dorsal and anal fins, as well as a much larger mouth, with a long lower jaw, the thickened tip of which fits into a depression in the upper jaw. In colour, the back is dark greenish, the sides silvery, the lower fins are deep red. There are no other species of *Aspius* in Europe, but there is one, *A. vorax* found in the basins of the Tigris and the Euphrates.

Habitat and distribution
The asp is usually found in the middle reaches of rivers in association with barbel or bream or in large lakes, and sometimes even in brackish water. Its distribution is from eastern Holland eastwards to the Southern Baltic and the Caspian, and south to the Danube basin and northwestern Turkey. Some of the populations in the Caspian and Black Seas are migratory, feeding in the estuaries and breeding upstream in fresh water.

Breeding and growth
The asp spawns in stony reaches of rivers in running water, the eggs being deposited over gravel in April or May.
Young fish swim in shoals, but adult specimens are usually solitary, reaching 40–60 cm (16–24 in) at four to five years, and a weight of up to 3.5 kg (8 lb). Very large specimens may be up to 120 cm (48 in) long and weigh 12 kg (27 lb).

Feeding
The asp feeds primarily on other cyprinid fish, especially bleak when mature, and on small crustaceans and other animals when young. The asp attacks a bleak shoal from below with a dashing lunge and a splash as it breaks the surface.

Fishing for asp
The asp is a valuable and popular sporting fish, because of its large size, sudden take and the good fight it puts up when hooked. In many ways its habits are similar to those of a large trout. It inhabits runs near bridges, weir pools, deep fast stretches, overgrown holes near the bank or deep pools on bends.
Baits are similar to those used for large trout. Small spoons can be effective, especially with some red wool attached to the hooks; they should be fished just below the surface. Live-baiting or dead-baiting with a small bleak is also recommended. Large flies and lures such as are used for rainbow trout in reservoirs have also been found to be successful, pale or even white flies, to imitate a small bleak, being the best.

Characteristics
Dorsal fin: 10 rays.
Anal fin: 12–14 branched rays.
Scales in lateral line: 65–74.
Pharyngeal teeth: 5 and 3 in two rows; smooth.

Asp from river Kokemaenjoki, Finland with Silverweed. Photographed 5 July.

Roach

Roach. *Rutilus rutilus* Linn. Family *Cyprinidae*. French, gardon;
German, Plötze; Swedish, mört; Dutch, blankvoorn; Finnish, särki.

Recognition and related species

Roach are silvery, rather deep-bodied fish, with red fins and eyes. Their
backs are generally greenish, with a silvery sheen, not golden as in rudd.
The front edge of the dorsal fin is in line with the base of the ventral,
which distinguishes them from rudd (p.86). Roach may be distinguished
from dace by their deeper body and by having fewer scales along the
lateral line, 42–45 in roach, 48–51 in dace. The orfe (p.84), which is also
rather similar has 56–61 scales along the lateral line.
Hybrids between roach and other species are common, especially the
roach-bream hybrid which may outnumber bream in some populations.
Hybrids are also recorded with rudd, chub, bleak and silver bream.

Habitat and distribution

Roach are probably the commonest fish in the lowland parts of the
British Isles. They are particularly tolerant of poor water quality and are
found in rivers, both clear and polluted, in lakes, ponds, gravel pits and
canals. Roach live both near the surface and in deep water; they may be
found in the higher reaches of rivers in company with trout, chub and
dace right down to the lower reaches with bream and bleak. They may
also be found in brackish water such as in the Baltic and in the Thames
estuary. In poor waters there may be large numbers of small fish, but in
others, such as Hornsea Mere and in rivers such as the river Beult in
Kent, good specimens are regularly caught.
Roach are common throughout southern and eastern England, but are
rarer in the north, in the West Country and in Wales. In Scotland they
are found only in the lowland areas of the south, northwards to the Tay.
In Ireland they have probably been introduced in historical times; they
were established first in the Blackwater in the south and the Erne and
Foyle rivers in the north, but are now spreading rapidly and replacing
the rudd.
On the Continent they are found from the Baltic, south to the Alps and
the Pyrenees, to the Balkans, north Turkey and the Caucasus and east to
the Urals.

Breeding and growth

Roach spawn in early summer, from April to June, attaching their eggs
to weeds. The success of spawning is very variable and is greatest in
warm summers. Rate of growth varies greatly according to habitat; in
poor acid waters the fish remain small and stunted, whereas in chalk
streams and other nutrient-rich running waters growth is at a maximum.
On average a one-year-old fish is around 5 cm (2 in) long, and a weight
of 500 gm (1 lb) is reached in nine to ten years; maximum age is about
twelve years, and the largest specimens are about 1.8 kg (4 lb). The
British record is 2.025 kg (4 lb 1 oz), caught by R. G. Jones in a gravel pit
in Nottinghamshire.

Feeding

Roach eat both animals and plant material, and the larger specimens
tend to become cannibal and take fry, no doubt often of their own
species. Roach-bream hybrids, which regularly grow large, seem
especially prone to cannibalism.

Fishing for roach

The roach is one of the most popular species for anglers, because it is so
common, and takes such a wide range of bait. Bread paste, crust or
worms are probably as good baits as any, as are all sorts of maggots. For
larger specimens, large baits should be used, and worms are probably
best; it is only for catching large numbers of small fish or in very heavily
fished waters that tiny hooks and delicate tackle are needed.
Roach are not normally eaten in England, but are used for food in some
parts of eastern Europe.

Characteristics

Dorsal fin: 10–11 rays.
Anal fin: 10–12 rays.
Scales along lateral line: 42–45.
Pharyngeal teeth: 5 or 6 in one row.

Small roach from river Wey. Photographed 12 November.

Filby Broad, Norfolk.

Roach from river Kennet, Berkshire. Photographed 29 November.

Lake Mustaselkä, Finland.

Orfe

Orfe or ide. *Leuciscus idus* Linn. Family *Cyprinidae*. French, ide melanote; German, Aland; Swedish, id; Dutch, winde; Finnish, sayne.

Recognition and related species

Although it belongs to the same genus as the chub, (*L. cephalus*), the orfe is very similar to the roach, but usually has a more golden sheen on the scales, and particularly in larger specimens, a broader, blunter head. It is more definitely distinguished by having 55–61 scales along the lateral line (42–5 in the roach), and by having the pharyngeal teeth in two rows, 5 large and 3 small. Chub are definitely less deep and broader fish, also with 44–6 scales along the lateral line.

Hybrids are reported between the orfe and the bream.

The golden orfe is a pale orange variety often seen as an ornamental in ponds and lakes. It is very hardy, and swims and feeds near the surface so that it does not make the water so muddy as do goldfish or carp.

Habitat and distribution

The orfe lives both in running water and in lakes, usually in lowland areas. It tends to prefer weedy areas of moderate depth such as the edges of reed-beds. It has done well and become established in some chalk streams in the south of England such as the Kennet, and in the river Annan in the Borders, but it is not native to the British Isles. Its native range extends from the Rhine eastwards to the Danube basin and north to Sweden, Finland and across Siberia. It is also found in brackish water in estuaries and in the Baltic.

Breeding and growth

Spawning takes place in April and May in shallow water among weed or stones.

Orfe grow to a larger size than roach, 30–40 cm (12–18 in) being common; the maximum is about 1 m (40 in) and a weight of about 4 kg (8¾ lb). The British rod-caught record is 1.913 kg (4 lb 3½ oz),

caught by D. R. Charles in the river Kennet in Berkshire in August 1983.

Feeding

Insects, both larvae and surface-living adults, form the usual food of orfe, together with snails and other invertebrates. Larger specimens also eat small fish.

Fishing for orfe

Because it takes bait freely and fights well when hooked, the orfe is popular with anglers in eastern Europe. Almost any bait is likely to be taken, e.g. small spinners, flies or baits such as worms, sweetcorn or bread paste. In Finland, where it is an important and widespread species, it is also commonly caught in gill nets.

Cooking orfe

In areas where it is common, e.g. in parts of Russia and in Finland the orfe is valued as a food fish. Its flesh is white, firm and of good flavour. It is marred by the presence of three-pronged bones similar to those found in the roach and bream (p.88), but they are fewer in number and more easily removed. Grilling, after the fish has been cleaned and de-scaled, is a good method of cooking, and it is best eaten with a delicately-flavoured sauce such as is made with mushrooms or herbs.

Characteristics

Dorsal fin: 8 rays.
Anal fin: 9–10 rays; concave.
Scales in lateral line: 55–61.
Pharyngeal teeth: 5 large 3 small in two rows.

Golden Orfe from the pond at Wisley Garden, Surrey.

Orfe from Lake Mustaselkä. Photographed 28 June.

85

Little Britain Lake, Middlesex.

Rudd

Rudd. *Scardinus erythrophthalmus* Linn. Family *Cyprinidae*. French, rotengle; German, Rotfeder; Swedish, sarv.

Recognition and related species

The rudd may be recognized by its deep body, with the scales on the back overlaid with a golden sheen, and bright red fins. It is most similar to the roach, but may be distinguished by the position of the dorsal fin; in rudd the front edge of the dorsal fin is behind the base of the ventral fin, in roach the front of the dorsal fin is level with the base of the ventral fin. Hybrids between roach and rudd are very difficult to identify without killing the fish and examining the pharyngeal teeth, which are in two rows in the rudd, but only in one row in the roach. Hybrids have also been recorded between rudd and bream.

Habitat and distribution

The rudd is found in canals, ponds, gravel pits and lakes, nearly always in still water and in areas with a good growth of weeds and reed beds. The Norfolk Broads are a typical habitat for good rudd.

In the British Isles rudd is common in southern England, but rarer in the north and almost absent from Scotland. In contrast to the roach, it is common throughout Ireland.

On the Continent the rudd is found from France and Italy north to Sweden and eastwards to western Siberia, northern Turkey and the Caspian.

Breeding and growth

The rudd spawns in early summer, from April to June, laying its eggs on water weeds. They grow at about the same rate as roach, reaching 500 gm (1 lb) in about ten years under normal conditions. Average size in England is 15–30 cm (6–12 in). The maximum weight is 2 kg (4–5 lb) and the British rod-caught record is 2.04 kg (4 lb 8 oz), caught by Rev. E. C. Alston at Thetford, Norfolk in 1933.

Feeding

The rudd feeds more on the surface than the roach, lying in shoals just under the surface in warm weather. It feeds on insects, both adults on the surface and larvae, and on some plant material, tending to lie near weedbeds or forage in beds of half-submerged reeds. In summer, larger specimens tend to eat fry of all sorts. The rudd continues to feed in warm water, when other species have ceased.

Fishing for rudd

Most methods used for taking roach will also be successful for rudd. On warm days when the fish are feeding on the surface they can be enticed to floating groundbait such as a crust of bread anchored on a raft or in a hairnet, and then fished for with a light float and a minimum of shot. Flies can also be successful, both wet and dry; for wet-fly a silver-bodied one such as a butcher is recommended, for dry a small black gnat or red ant is effective, especially if baited with a single maggot. Alternatively maggots can be cast with a fly rod and line and allowed to sink gently among the fish.

Rudd are not commonly eaten in England, but are farmed for food in parts of Europe, and are occasionally seen in fish markets, even in London.

Characteristics

Dorsal fin: 9–10 rays. Anal fin: 11–12 rays.
Scales along the lateral line: 40–45.
Pharyngeal teeth: 5 large and 3 smaller in two rows.

Rudd from Little Britain Lake, Middlesex. Photographed 14 July.

River Thames at Hurley, Berkshire.

Common bream

Common bream, bronze bream. *Abramis brama* Linn. Family
Cyprinidae. French, brême; German, Brachsen; Swedish, braxen;
Dutch, brasen; Finnish, lahna.

Recognition and related species

The bream is a deep fish with very slimy skin and dark brown fins. When
young the body is silvery, but it becomes darker and more golden-olive
with age. Its deeply forked tail with pointed lobes and anal fin with more
than 25 rays is characteristic. The dorsal fin is set well back, to the rear of
the pelvic fins. The most similar fish to the common bream is the silver
bream, which has larger scales, 44–8 along the lateral line, less than 25
rays in the anal fin, and a very short snout. In adult common bream the
length of the snout is longer than the diameter of the eye.

Roach × bream hybrids are common, especially where the water
contains many roach and few bream. They are characterized by reddish
fins like a roach, but a longer anal fin and a deeper body with more
abundant slime. These hybrids may be fertile, so when they occur in any
number, backcrosses may be expected, which will be nearer to either of
the parent species.

Small bream or skimmer from Boulder Mere, Surrey.

Habitat and distribution

Bream are characteristic fish of rich lowland lakes and slow-flowing
rivers and canals. They are plentiful throughout England, and in the
central plain of Ireland. On the Continent, bream are found in the Baltic,
in both brackish and fresh water, southwards to the Alps and Pyrenees,
and through the Balkans to northern Turkey and the Caucasus, then
eastwards to the Urals, the central Asian steppes and the Aral sea.

Feeding

Bream are primarily bottom-feeding fish, moving in shoals and nosing in
the mud with an extendible mouth. They feed on insect larvae, molluscs
and worms; larger specimens become predatory, and take small fish.
Shoals of feeding fish can sometimes be found by spotting an area where
the mud has been churned up. Each shoal consists of fish of more or less
the same size and age. Feeding is most active in summer and autumn.

Breeding and growth

Bream spawn from May to July, the eggs being laid on water weeds. The
average adult size is 25–45 cm (10–16 in), though the largest specimens
may be 80 cm (32 in) and weigh over 8.5 kg (19 lb). The British record is
6.24 kg (13 lb 12 oz), caught by A. Smith in a gravel pit in Oxfordshire,
1983, and several specimens from 5.5–6 kg (12–13 lb) are recorded.
Growth is usually slow, a length of 10 cm (4 in) being reached in two to

three years, and 45 cm (16 in), 2.25 kg (4½ lb) after eleven years.
Because bream, in the British Isles, are at the northern end of their
range, spawning is most successful in warm summers, and annual
survival is 50–60%.

Fishing for bream

Liberal ground baiting is supposed to be one of the prime requirements
in successful bream fishing. Once a shoal has been located or attracted,
sport may continue for some time in the same place, as long as the fish
are not frightened. Many baits are successful, but bread paste is
probably the best; small worms or maggots enclosed in a ball of soft mud
and fished on the bottom, are also recommended. In *Stillwater Angling*
Richard Walker reports that an angler at Graffham, fishing a large white
lure on a sunk line, caught two bream over 4.5 kg (10 lb); large
specimens could probably be taken regularly with a lure or light spoon.
Though regularly eaten in Europe, the bream is not usually considered
edible in Britain; we found the flesh soft, of pleasant but slight flavour,
but ruined by hundreds of unavoidable three-pronged bones.

Characteristics

Dorsal fin: 12 rays. Anal fin: 25–31 rays.
Scales along the lateral line: 51–60. Pharyngeal teeth: 5 in one row.

Bream from Claydon Lake, Buckinghamshire, living in muddy water. Photographed 19 June.

Bream from Lake Jaminginselkä, Finland, living in clear peaty water. Photographed 27 June.

Sixteen foot drain, Cambridgeshire.

Silver bream

Silver bream. *Blicca bjoerkna* Linn. Family *Cyprinidae*. French, brême bordelière; German, Güster; Swedish, björkna; Dutch, kolblei. Old English names: white bream or breamflat.

Recognition and related species

The silver bream is very similar to its much commoner relative the common bream, but its body is always silvery and never golden-olive. Small specimens of both, however, are silvery, but differ also in several minor features: the silver bream has 44–8 scales along the lateral line, the common 51–60 scales along the lateral line. The silver bream has 19–24 rays in the anal fin, the common 23–30 rays. The silver bream also has a shorter snout; the distance between the tip of the snout and the eye is less than or equal to the diameter of the eye. In the common bream the distance between the tip of the snout and the eye is greater than the diameter of the eye.

Hybrids have recently been recorded between the silver bream and the common or bronze bream, and between silver bream and roach, in Lincolnshire, where the silver bream is common. Hybrids have also been recorded on the Continent between silver bream and rudd.

Habitat and distribution

The silver bream occurs in the same habitats as the common bream – lowland lakes, canals and slow-flowing rivers – but is much rarer. It is commonest in Lincolnshire, between the Humber and the Wash and in East Anglia and is otherwise scattered through the Midlands and southern England.

On the Continent, the silver bream is found around the Baltic, southwards to the Alps, the Balkans and the Caucasus, and eastwards to the Volga.

Breeding and growth

Silver bream spawn in still water from May to July, laying their eggs on water weeds. Growth is moderate: after one year the young fish are 6–8 cm (2½–3 in) long. Adult length of 20–25 cm (8–10 in) is reached in about eight years in England. The maximum length of 36 cm (14½ in) is exceptional. Fish over 500 gm (1 lb) are distinctly rare.

Feeding

Silver bream eat small animals and plants. They feed both on the bottom and in mid-water.

Fishing for silver bream

The methods used for common bream should also be appropriate for silver bream, but as they are always smaller and useless for food, they are not highly regarded by anglers either here or on the Continent.

Characteristics

Dorsal fin: 8–9 rays.
Anal fin: 19–24 rays, usually 22.
Scales along the lateral line: (40–) (43–49) (–51).
Pharyngeal teeth: 5 large and 2 small in two rows.

Silver bream from Peasgate Pond, near Spilsby, Lincolnshire. Photographed 1 December.

Lake Jaminginselkä, Finland.

Blue bream

Blue bream. *Abramis ballerus* Linn. Family *Cyprinidae*. German, Zope; Swedish, faren; Finnish, sulkava; Russian, sinetz.

Recognition and related species

The blue bream is similar to the common bream, but is darker and greyer in colour, especially on the back, and less deep in shape; its mouth is distinctly superior, the lower lip curving upwards and appearing longer than the lower. Other differences are in the number of scales along the lateral line, 66–73 in blue bream, 51–60 in common bream, and in the number of rays in the anal fin (39–46 as against 24–30). The silver bream (p.90) has even fewer scales and rays in the anal fin. A third species the Danubian or Whiteye Bream (*Abramis sapa* Pallas) is found in the lower Danube and in eastern Europe north of the Black and Caspian seas. It has a silvery-grey body, but differs from the blue bream in having 49–52 scales in the lateral line, and a distinctly inferior mouth.

Habitat and distribution

The lower reaches of rivers and lowland lakes are the typical habitat of the blue bream. It is an adaptable fish and able to take advantage of reservoirs constructed on rivers, and is actively spreading northwards, for example in Finland as the lakes become more eutrophic or polluted. It is therefore regarded as a pest, being almost useless and frequently caught in nets intended for more valuable species, e.g. whitefish. The distribution of the blue bream at present extends from southern Finland and Sweden to northern Germany, south to the Black and Caspian seas and along the lower Danube. It is usually found in fresh water, but is also found in brackish water in the Baltic, Black and Caspian seas.

Breeding and growth

Spawning takes place from April to June depending on the latitude. The eggs are laid on weeds or on gravel in shallow water.

The usual size of the blue bream is between 30 and 40 cm (12 and 16 in); the maximum about 45 cm (18 in). Males are usually larger than females.

Feeding

Blue bream are plankton feeders living in shoals in open water, and so competing, in northern waters, with whitefish and vendace.

Fishing for blue bream

Because it is smaller and inhabits the same waters as the common bream, the blue bream is less valued by anglers. It is not a bottom feeder, but it should be possible to catch it with small baits such as maggots or ant-pupae, fished in mid-water. The specimens we photographed here were taken in gill nets intended for whitefish.

Cooking blue bream

In the northern part of its range the blue bream is regarded as useless, fit food only for gulls, but in the lower basins of the Volga and Danube in southeastern Europe it is eaten salted or dried to accompany vodka or beer.

Characteristics

Dorsal fin: 8–9 rays.
Anal fin: 36–43 rays.
Scales in the lateral line: 66–73.
Pharyngeal teeth: 5 in one row.

Blue bream from Lake Jamınginselkä. Photographed 27 June.

Gudgeon from river Ouzel, Bedfordshire, with leaves of giant butterbur. Photographed 20 October.

Gudgeon

Gudgeon. *Gobio gobio* Linn. Family *Cyprinidae*. French, goujon; German, Gründling; Swedish, sandkrypare; Dutch, riviergrondel.

Recognition and related species
This small slender fish is usually found in large shoals in slow-flowing and often muddy streams and rivers. It is recognized by its silvery body with darker patches, and its two small barbels at the back of the mouth. Small barbel are most likely to be confused with gudgeon, but they have four barbels and are unmarked. The southern barbel is much more heavily marked than the gudgeon and has four barbels even longer than those of the common barbel.

Habitat and distribution
The gudgeon is found most commonly in the middle reaches of rivers, usually on gravelly shallows where there is a reasonable flow, but it is also frequent in canals and lakes. In lowland areas such as Lincolnshire it is found in all sections of river except the uppermost, where it is replaced by the bullhead. The faster-flowing stretches contain the larger gudgeon. It can survive in brackish water, being found in the Thames estuary around London and in the less salty parts of the Baltic.
In winter the shoals move into deeper water. It is common in England, particularly in the south and in the midlands, but rare in Scotland. It has a wide distribution from Ireland and southern Sweden to southern France and eastwards across Europe and central Asia to China and the Pacific.

Breeding and growth
The gudgeon spawns early summer, in May and June, usually on gravelly shallows. Growth is fairly slow, the normal maximum length of around 15 cm (6 in) being reached in three years. In a large population netted in Buckinghamshire in October 1983, gudgeon of 11 cm and 13 cm (4½ and 5 in) were the commonest sizes, representing possibly two- and three-year-old adults, out of many hundreds there were no fish larger than 15 cm (6 in). The British rod-caught record is 120 gm (4 oz 4 drm), caught by M. J. Bowen in Ebbw Vale, Wales.

Feeding
Gudgeon feed mainly on the bottom, and take all kinds of insect larvae, crustaceans and worms.

Fishing for gudgeon
Gudgeon are free-biting fish and take a variety of baits, though maggots and small worms fished on the bottom are probably the most successful. Nowadays they are not often fished for their own sake, but may be caught as bait for larger fish, notably pike, or to boost the matchman's catch when the larger species are not taking. In the nineteenth century gudgeon fishing picnics by punt were very popular on the Thames. The practice was to rake an area of gravelly shallows about one metre (three feet) deep to attract the fish and bring them on the feed, as is sometimes done with tench or grayling; fast and productive sport could then be expected, with delicate tackle, and a small red worm as bait. Hot sunny weather seemed to make the fish hungrier, which was no doubt a contribution to the success of the picnic. Gudgeon are reported to be delicate and delicious in flavour, but need careful cleaning, especially if they come from polluted water. The smaller ones may be eaten like whitebait, the larger fried or grilled like a fresh sardine.

Characteristics
Dorsal fin: 9–10 rays. Anal fin: 8 rays. Scales in the lateral line: 38–44. Pharyngeal teeth: 5 and 2 or 3 smaller in two rows.

River Ouzel, Bedfordshire.

Claydon Lake, Buckinghamshire.

Common carp

Common carp. *Cyprinus carpio* Linn. Family *Cyprinidae*. French, carpe; German, Karpe; Swedish, karp; Dutch, karper.

Recognition and related species

Carp have been valued and cultivated for many thousands of years, and some of the many varieties are mentiond below. All common carp can be recognized by their very long-based dorsal fins with *c*. 20 rays, and the single pair of barbels at the mouth. Gudgeon also have a single pair of barbels, but have a short-based dorsal fin. Barbels have two pairs of barbels as well as a short-based dorsal. Crucian carp (see p.102) and goldfish (p.100) also have a long-based dorsal fin, but have no barbels. The carp has been domesticated for many thousand years and several varieties have been selected on the Continent for their fast growth and lack of scales.

Two typical forms of these are the leather carp, which has no or very few large scales, and the mirror carp, which has one or two rows of large scales along its sides or a scatter of scales. A percentage of the progeny of these few-scaled forms will be fully scaled, but also deep-bodied and fast-growing. These fast-growing forms are collectively known as 'king' carp, but the term 'king' seems sometimes to include the leather and mirror forms, sometimes to refer only to the fully-scaled form. King carp are distinguishable from 'wild' carp by their deeper bodies, generally fatter appearance and faster growth. Where both types, king and wild carp are present, they are likely to interbreed, and become indistinguishable.

Hybrids are reported between common carp and crucian carp; they look like goldfish, but have very small barbels.

Habitat and distribution

Carp are typically a species of rich weedy ponds and lakes. In shallow water they will root around on the bottom and stir up much mud thus inhibiting the growth of submerged weeds, but water-lilies and other strong-growing weeds with floating leaves are not affected. Carp also live in slow rivers, especially in southern Europe and western Asia, but also in rivers such as the Thames and Trent, even into tidal and brackish water.

In the British Isles the carp is commonest in the south-east, indeed it is only here that the summers are warm enough for it to breed. It is found also in scattered localities in Ireland. The carp is not native in the British Isles. It was introduced from Europe, probably in the late Middle Ages, and kept as a food fish, especially in monastic fish ponds. The exact date of its introduction into England is unknown, but Dame Juliana Berners mentioned carp in 1486: 'a daynteous fusshe, but there ben but few in Englonde, and thereforre I wryte the lesse of hym'.

The carp was originally native in eastern Europe and western Asia, probably from the Danube eastwards to the northern Caspian and Aral seas, but today it is found in all the countries of western Europe, excluding northern Scandinavia, and throughout Turkey and Israel. It has been introduced also to the East, notably India, as well as to America, Australia, South Africa, etc.

Breeding and growth

Carp spawn when the water temperature exceeds 18°C (64°F) which in Britain is from late May until early June depending on the season. A warm season is necessary for successful spawning.

The females lay numerous eggs, around two million have been

Carp from Claydon Lake, Buckinghamshire. Photographed 4 November.

Lake in Rhône valley, France.

calculated to be produced by a 7.25 kg (16½ lb) fish, and these are laid at intervals among weeds in shallow water, 20–40 cm (8–16 in) deep, the males at the same time showing themselves with much leaping and splashing.

Growth is very fast when food is plentiful and the water warm. Cultivated carp may reach 1 kg (2 lb) in a year, and easily put on 1 kg (2 lb) each year after that. Richard Walker's record 20 kg (44 lb) carp caught in Redmire Pool, Herefordshire, in 1952 was found to be fifteen years old. The maximum possible weight is probably much greater than this. Alwyne Wheeler records a specimen weighing 32 kg (70 lb 8 oz) from Italy in 1886.

Carp are famous for their longevity, but definite records are hard to come by. The record 20 kg (44 lb) fish was kept after its capture in London Zoo where it survived until 1972. Stories that the carp fed by Marie Antoinette at Versailles may still be fed today are certainly apocryphal. As Sir Herbert Maxwell wrote in *British Freshwater Fishes* (1904) they 'are believed to have shared the fate of other privileged classes at the hands of the revolutionaries in 1790'.

Feeding

Carp are omnivorous, feeding on invertebrates of all kinds, on weed and on algae. Insect larvae, shrimps and freshwater mussels are favourites, the latter eaten whole in their shells. They probably also eat small fish on occasion.

Water temperature has an important effect on their feeding, and they seldom feed at temperatures above 20°C (68°F) or below 14°C (57°F). They tend also to feed better when the oxygen content of the water is higher, e.g. in shallow water or in warm windy weather.

Fishing for carp

Carp are by nature among the most wary of freshwater fish, and big specimens have had ample time to become wily. Because of their large size and the powerful fight they put up when hooked, they are popular with anglers who take the necessary trouble to catch them. Many books have been written on carp fishing and Richard Walker's own writings on the subject are especially valuable. Some of his main recommendations are to use as soft a line as possible at the hook so that the fish do not feel the resistance associated with stiff nylon, and to vary the bait to something that other anglers have not been using; carp will eat almost any of the usual baits but soon become wary of any particular one. The angler should be inventive, trying new baits and combinations of bait which will entice the carp, but which they will not associate with danger. Careful groundbaiting with any new bait will be necessary before the carp have developed a taste for it. Early morning and evening are the best times in warm weather, though in hot weather the carp will feed best at night when the water is cool, and in cold weather will feed through the day.

Mirror carp from Wisley Gardens, Surrey. Photographed 18 October.

Leather carp from Great Stambridge Fishery, Essex. Photographed 4 December.

Cooking carp

Carp are not popular food fish in England, where there has always been an abundance of fresh seafish, but are very popular on the Continent, especially in eatern Europe, and in China. The flesh is firm and white, of good flavour provided that the fish has not been living in too stagnant a pond.

Recipes usually include a good quantity of herbs and wine. Carp is also very good in curry, and popular in parts of India. When it is eaten with the fingers the sharp bones can be detected more easily.

Characteristics

Dorsal fin: 17–21 rays, the first bony and serrated.
Anal fin: 10 rays.
Scales in the lateral line: 33–40.
Pharyngeal teeth: 3, 1, and 1 in three rows.

Sheffield Park Lake, Sussex.

Goldfish

Goldfish. *Carassius auratus* Linn. Family *Cyprinidae*. French, poisson rouge; German, Goldfisch; Swedish, gulfisk; Dutch, goudvis.

Recognition and related species

The goldfish is familiar to everyone as it is the most popular domesticated fish. The fat body, long fins and overall bright orange colour of the commonest forms are easy to recognize, even when the odd escaped specimen is seen in the wild in the company of other fish.

The only other common orange-bodied fish is the golden orfe (p.84), but it usually has a more slender body and has a short-based dorsal fin. Less common, but very similar to the goldfish, is the golden carp, a form of the common carp; like the common carp it has barbels which are absent in the goldfish. There is also a golden form of the tench, but it has the other tench-characters, a long rounded dorsal fin and many very small scales.

A non-golden subspecies is sometimes found, the gibel carp or Prussian carp, and non-gold young can be produced by golden parents. They closely resemble crucian carp (indeed the two belong to the same genus) but have fewer scales along the lateral line, and the first dorsal fin ray is strongly serrated (only weakly serrated in the crucian). These are probably close to the wild type from which the goldfish was bred.

Habitat and distribution

Ponds, lakes and slow-flowing rivers are suitable for goldfish; they are particularly hardy and can tolerate both high and low temperatures, and so can survive in small garden pools.

Goldfish are native of eastern Asia, probably originating in northern China and Korea. Korea was probably the country where they were first domesticated, but their culture was taken up in China and Japan and many fancy forms, with round bodies, telescope eyes, very long fins or no scales were produced. They were first introduced into England in the seventeenth century, but seldom bred here, being imported in large numbers from Portugal.

Because of their popularity as pets, goldfish are now found throughout Europe. The Prussian carp, *C. auratus gibelio* is probably native in eastern Europe and into Siberia.

Breeding and growth

In order to spawn successfully, goldfish need a temperature of 21°C (70°F) though they will lay eggs at a lower temperature. The eggs are laid on waterweed near the surface of the water.

Growth varies greatly with temperature and food supply. By the end of their first year the young are about 6 cm (2½ in) long. Maximum size is about 45 cm (16 in) and a weight of about 3 kg (6.5 lb). Cultivated specimens may live to be thirty years old.

Feeding

Goldfish eat both aquatic invertebrates, such as *Daphnia*, and some plant matter.

Goldfish. Photographed 1 December.

Characteristics

Dorsal fin: 16–19 rays, concave.
Anal fin: 8 rays.
Scales in the lateral line: 27–31.
Pharyngeal teeth: 4 in one row.

'King' carp from Seven Acres Pond, Wisley. Photographed 19 October.

Boulder Mere, Surrey.

Crucian carp

Crucian carp. *Carassius carassius* Linn. Family *Cyprinidae*. French, carassin; German, Karausche; Swedish, ruda.

Recognition and related species

The crucian carp is a deep-bodied fish with rounded fins and is usually a deep golden-brown colour. It is distinguished from the common carp by its lack of barbels and deeper body, and from other barbel-less carps by its long straight dorsal fin with 14–21 rays. The goldfish is the most similar, and belongs to the same genus, but differs in having less than 31 scales along the lateral line, and a concave dorsal fin, as well as being less deep in the body.

Habitat and distribution

Crucian carp are very tolerant of poorly-oxygenated water, and weedy, stagnant and shaded pools, and these, together with slow flowing rivers and canals, are its usual habitat.

It is probably not native to England, but was introduced because it does well in poorer, more acid or muddier pools where the common carp would not thrive. It is now found mainly in the south-east of England, in the Weald, in East Anglia and in the Midlands. On the Continent it is found from Sweden and Germany, southwards to northern Italy and eastwards to Siberia.

Breeding and growth

The crucian carp spawns in May and June. The small yellow eggs, 1.5 mm (¹⁄₁₆ in) in diameter, are laid on weeds. It is more tolerant of cold than the common carp, being able to spawn in water at 14°C (57°F) and above, while the common carp requires 18°C (64°F) or more before successful spawning can take place.

The average length of adults is 15–25 cm (6–10 in), and a weight of about 250 gm (8 oz). A specimen over 1 kg (2 lb) is a good fish, and the British rod-caught record is 2.565 kg (5 lb 10 oz), caught by G. Halls near Kings Lynn in 1976. On the Continent the maximum recorded is about 50 cm (20 in).

Hybrids with common carp are found where the two species live together. They resemble the crucian, but often have small barbels, and are less deep in the body. Nearly all the hybrids are males.

Feeding

Plants, insect larvae and other small aquatic animals are the usual food of crucian carp.

Fishing for crucian carp

The crucian is considered the poor cousin of the common carp, as it neither grows to such a large size, nor fights so strongly. It is strictly a bottom feeder, and has a reputation for being a very gentle biter, so delicate tackle should be used. Baits such as bread paste, small worms and maggots are all suitable, and warm evenings in summer the best time.

The crucian carp is not highly regarded as a food fish, although it is cultivated for food in some parts of Europe.

Characteristics

Dorsal fin: 14–21 branched rays, 1 spine on leading edge.
Anal fin: 6–8 branched rays, 1 spine on leading edge.
Pharyngeal teeth: 4 in one row.

Crucian carp from Boulder Mere. Photographed 11 November.

Pond at Shinfield, Berkshire.

Grass carp

Grass carp. *Ctenopharyngodon idella* Valenciennes. Family *Cyprinidae*.
German, Graeskarpe.

Recognition and related species

Although it is called a carp, this fish more closely resembles a chub with its elongated body, silver scales with a golden sheen, and few-rayed fins. It has a large and very wide mouth, with 43–45 scales along the lateral line. All the fins are rounded, and the anal fin has eight branched rays. The front edges of the dorsal and ventral fins are in line.

Habitat and distribution

The grass carp is native of eastern China and Russia and is found in the Amur river and in Chinese rivers south of it. It has been introduced into ponds and navigation and drainage channels to control excessive weed growth. It is being stocked experimentally in a few places in southern England, in East Anglia and in Lincolnshire, but as it is unlikely to be able to breed, there is little danger of its spreading. It has also been introduced into several parts of south-eastern Europe.

Breeding and growth

Grass carp spawn in fast stretches of rivers, the eggs being carried many miles downstream on the current before hatching.
Grass carp grow very large at a fast rate, finally reaching 1.25 m (4 ft) and a weight of *c*. 35 kg (77 lb).

Feeding

Fry feed on animal plankton such as *Daphnia*, but as soon as they are about 2–5 cm (1–2 in) in length, the fish feed entirely on plants and it is because of this it is of use in clearing weed.

Fishing for grass carp

Such a large fish would make a potentially valuable quarry for the angler; although it is unlikely that the huge weights recorded elsewhere would be achieved in cooler west European waters, specimens of 4.5 kg (10 lb) and upwards have been grown in England. The British rod-caught record is 4.42 kg (9 lb 12 oz), caught by G. A. Gwilt at Trawsfynydd Lake, Gwynedd, North Wales in 1983.

Characteristics

Dorsal fin: 8 rays.
Anal fin: 8 rays.
Scales in the lateral line: 43–45.
Pharyngeal teeth: 4 or 5, and 2 in two rows.

Grass carp from Reading University experimental pond, Berkshire.

Cowley Lake, Middlesex.

Tench

Tench. *Tinca tinca* Linn. Family *Cyprinidae*. French, tanche; German, Schleie; Swedish, sutane; Dutch, zeelt.

Recognition and related species
The tench is easily recognized by its minute scales, which give it an almost scale-less appearance, by its rounded fins and almost unforked tail. In colour it is dark olive or blackish, depending on the water from which it came. The mouth has one pair of small barbels. Another characteristic feature is the thick 'wrist' of the tail, much thicker than in most other fish. Males and females may be distinguished by their ventral fins, short and rounded in the female, longer, more pointed and reaching up to the vent in the males. There is a golden form of tench with orange skin and irregular dark spots, and a rare variety mentioned by Richard Walker, known as the vermilion tench, with greenish sides and a deep-orange belly. He also records that in clear waters, such as flooded chalk pits, tench may have brassy-gold sides, white bellies and red fins. There are no records of hybrids involving tench, and no other closely related species in Europe.

Habitat and distribution
The tench is typically a fish of deep muddy, weedy waters, ponds, lakes or canals; it lives mainly on the bottom, and especially near beds of bullrushes (*Scirpus*) but may be seen near the surface when spawning, and at night. It is very tolerant of low oxygen, and can bury itself in the mud and hibernate in winter. Tench are common throughout south-east England, south of the Humber, but are rarer in Scotland and Wales; in Ireland they are found mostly in the central plain. On the Continent they are very widespread, being found throughout western Europe, including Spain eastwards to central Siberia.

Breeding and growth
Tench spawn in summer, from May to July, laying their eggs among water weeds, *Potamogeton* apparently being especially favoured. Wild tench rarely reach more than 2 kg (4 lb), but large specimens up to 8.5 kg (17½ lb) are known. The British rod-caught record is 4.6 kg (10 lb 1 oz) from Wilstone Reservoir, Herts, caught by A. J. Chester in 1981. Many fish of 4 kg (7–8 lb) have been caught recently.

Feeding
Tench feed mainly on aquatic invertebrates such as insect larvae and worms, and they also eat some plant material. When feeding they send up strings of very small bubbles, and these are a good indication of where the tench are.

Fishing for tench
The tench is a favourite angling species, particularly for the specimen fisher rather than the matchman. The best chances of success are in the evening and early morning in warm weather in summer, and the fish often continue to feed throughout the night; however, like most fish, they will continue to feed all day in cooler or cloudy weather. Most of the usual baits may be used for tench, but bread paste or crust and lobworms are probably as good as any. Richard Walker recommends bread, and reports that tench have often been caught at night on floating crust meant for carp. He also describes in detail the behaviour of the tench in feeding head down on the bottom, unable to get hold of the bait because it fans it away with its fins, as it attempts to take it, giving the angler the impression that the tench is playing with the bait, or just shy or capricious. For this reason, or if the angler suspects this might be happening, it is advisable to have at least 60 cm (2 ft) between the shot and the bait, so that the float and line are far enough from the bait to be unaffected by the tench's waving tail.

Cooking tench
As a food fish the tench deserves more attention than it usually gets in Britain. Sir Herbert Maxwell quotes Ausonius the 'distinguished administrator' writing in his tenth idyll, about the Moselle (*c.* AD 385): 'Who has not heard of green tench, a favourite of the peasants, or bleak, the quarry for boys' hooks, or the shad, sizzling on the townspeople's grill?'
Maxwell also describes an excellent dish of small tenches delicately fried in oil, eaten for lunch at the wayside tavern in Meury-sur-Loire, his appetite no doubt heightened by having cycled from Orléans.
Today tench are commonly cultivated in carp ponds in eastern Europe, and occasionally sold in fishmongers in London.

Characteristics
Dorsal fin: 10–12 rays.
Anal fin: 9–10 rays.
Scales in the lateral line: 95–120.
Pharyngeal teeth: 4 or 5 in one row.

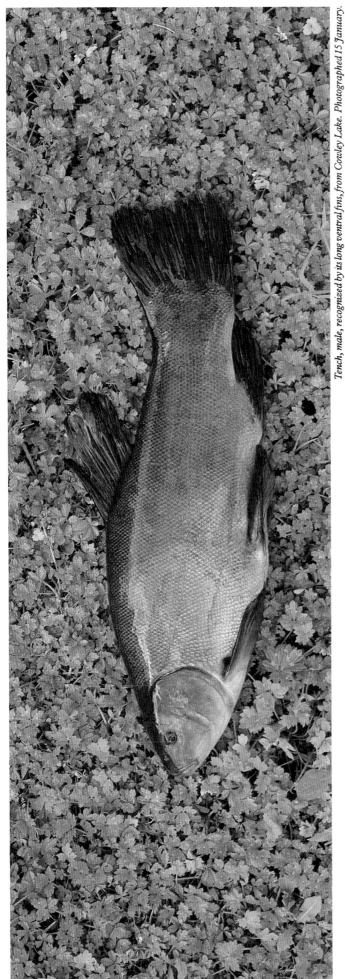

Tench, male, recognized by its long ventral fins, from Cowley Lake. Photographed 15 January.

Tench, female, from Cowley Lake. Photographed 8 July.

Claydon Lake, Buckinghamshire.

Wels or catfish

Wels or catfish. *Silurus glanis* Linn. Family *Siluridae*. French, silure glane; German, Waller or Wels; Swedish, mal; Dutch, meerval; Finnish, monni.

Recognition and related species
The wels is easily recognized by its huge wide mouth with six long soft feelers and its elongated tapering body with one very small dorsal fin. The anal fin, however, is very long, extending for about half the total length of the fish. No related species are found in northern Europe. The only other European species is Aristotle's catfish, (*S. aristotelis*), which is confined to the basin of the Akheloos river on the mainland of Greece opposite Corfu. It has only two long and two short barbels, and reaches a mere 150 kg (370 lb). A third species (*S. triostegus*) is known in the Tigris and Euphrates.

Other catfish found in Europe are introductions from America; the black bullhead (p.110) is easily distinguished by being small, (20–30 cm/ 8–12 in) with a normal size dorsal and anal fin, an adipose fin, and eight feelers around the mouth.

The wels is of remarkably similar shape and appearance to the burbot (p.118). They are unrelated, but share the same type of habitat, the wels being a more southern fish. Burbot may be distinguished by having only one feeler, by having modified ventral fins near the head, and by its very long second dorsal (absent in wels).

Habitat and distribution
The wels is found in rich lakes and large slow-flowing rivers. It also lives in brackish water in the southern Baltic, Black Sea and Caspian. It lives mostly on the bottom, being primarily a scavenger or predator of fish, but there are reports of it rising to the surface to attack swimming animals such as ducks or even dogs.

The ninth Duke of Bedford was probably responsible for the successful introduction of the wels to two lakes at Woburn in 1880. Seventy small specimens were said to have been put in, and it is probable that the present stock is descended from them. This was not the first introduction, as in 1865 fourteen were brought into the country by the Acclimatization Society.

At present catfish are found in several lakes in central England, e.g. at Woburn Abbey, at Claydon, some gravel pits near Leighton Buzzard, at Tring, and possibly some rivers such as the Wissey, from which a 7.5 kg (17 lb) specimen was reported to have been taken in 1953.

On the Continent, wels are native from the Danube eastwards to the Aral Sea and the Oxus. They have been introduced into France and Germany as well as to England.

Breeding and growth
The male opens out a depression in the bottom, and the eggs are laid in a large sticky pile by the female and guarded by the male until they hatch; one female may lay half a million eggs. Spawning usually takes place between May and July when the water temperature reaches 19°C (66°F). The young mature after four to five years, and may live up to twenty or even thirty years. A seven-year-old fish may weigh between 1.5 and 7 kg (3 and 15 lb).

The maximum size recorded in England is around 33 kg (73 lb) and the British rod-caught record is 19.73 kg (43½ lb), caught by R. J. Bray in Wilstone Reservoir, Tring, Herts in 1970. On the Continent the wels grow much larger, reaching a maximum of 3 m (nearly 10 ft) and a weight of 299 kg (440 lb), and there is an old record of a specimen from the Dneiper of 5 m (16½ ft) and 306 kg (675 lb).

Feeding
Young fish eat small invertebrates, but larger ones are predators and scavengers, eating small fish, large shellfish and waterfowl.

Fishing for catfish
Because of their great size, potentially the heaviest freshwater fish resident in the British Isles (only the sturgeon may be bigger), catfish are a popular species with anglers. They put up a powerful fight when hooked, and they are neither too easy nor too difficult to catch.

Tackle should be powerful, similar to that used for large carp, and a line with a minimum of 5 kg (11 lb) should be used, with a powerful carp hook, at least size no. 3.

Many different baits have proved successful at Claydon lakes which are well stocked with large catfish. Herring pieces, sprats and other dead fish, such as the tail sections of trout, squid heads, frogs, freshwater mussels, large bunches of worms, even pieces of kidney and chicken guts. Live bait may also be successful, and crucian carp are specially recommended as bait in Germany.

Catfish are said to be nocturnal, but may be caught at all times of day, though morning and evening are probably best.

When hooked the fish may make a preliminary long run, often a bolt for cover, so a reel holding plenty of line is required. After that the fish mostly keeps near the bottom, fighting hard until tired out. On the bank, wels are remarkably quiet, seeming to wait patiently while the hooks are removed, but slipping away fast once returned to the water.

Cooking wels
We have not had the opportunity to sample wels ourselves, but they are said to be good to eat, especially when smoked, though with a tendency to be greasy.

On the Continent, e.g. Hungary, they are often kept in fish farms, and marketed at 3.4 kg (8 lb) for food.

Characteristics
Dorsal fin: 4 rays, very small. Anal fin: very long-based, narrow, *c.* 75 rays. Barbels: 2 very long, 4 shorter. Scales absent.

Wels from Claydon Lake. Photographed 19 June.

American catfish, black bullhead

American catfish, black bullhead, horned pout. *Ictalurus melas* Raf. Family *Ictaluridae*. French, poisson chat; German, Zwergurels; Dutch, dwergmeerval; Finnish, piikkimonni.

Recognition and related species

This catfish was introduced from North America into Europe in the nineteenth century and has spread, and in some places bred, very prolifically. It is easily recognized by the eight long but unequal feelers around its mouth, and by the adipose fin similar to that found in the salmon family.

One other closely-related species is found in Europe, the American brown bullhead, *Ictalurus nebulosus*. This is generally browner and is mottled with black; it has well-developed barbs on the spine on the pectoral fins, and 21–4 rays in these anal fins. The black bullhead has no barbs, and only 17–21 rays. The brown bullhead is commonest in Holland and Belgium.

Other species may possibly appear in Europe, notably *I. punctatus*, the channel catfish which is spotted, as its Latin name suggests.

Habitat and distribution

The most likely places to find the American catfish are in still or sluggish waters near large rivers, gravel pits, canals or ponds, especially where the water is warm and weedy.

They have become pests in places in southern Europe, notably in the Rhône valley from where our specimens were caught. They are naturalized also in Germany and Italy and in central Europe.

Breeding and growth

Spawning takes place in summer. The eggs are laid in a nest among stones, logs or other cover, where they remain in a lump and are guarded and fanned by both parents; the fry also remain in a tight shoal for the first few days of their life.

Average adult length is 20–30 cm (8–12 in) but specimens as large as 61 cm (24 in) have been recorded.

Feeding

These catfish eat worms, crustaceans, small fish and plants.

Fishing for catfish

Any type of bait is suitable for these greedy fish. They are said to be easy to catch, especially on worms. Care should be taken with the brown bullhead if encountered because of its barbed and spiny pectoral fins which have poisonous glands at their base. We have had no experience of eating these fish; the brown bullhead is said to have tasty but greasy flesh.

Characteristics

Dorsal fin: 7 rays.
Anal fin: 17–21 rays.
Scales absent.

Bitterling

Bitterling. *Rhodeus sericeus* Bloch. Family *Cyprinidae*. French, bouviére; German, Bitterling; Dutch, bitter voorn.

Recognition and related species

The bitterling is a small, rather deep fish, in general outline like a very small crucian carp, but it is silvery rather than golden and has fewer (8–9 versus 14–21) rays in the dorsal fin. In the spawning season the males become very brightly coloured with a pinkish flush and a bright blue streak near the tail. The anal fin is also rather long-based, with about eleven rays. The lateral line is incomplete and confined to the first six scales.

There are no closely related species in Europe.

Habitat and distribution

The bitterling is found in slow-flowing lowland rivers, canals, rich lakes and ponds, all of which provide a suitable habitat for the freshwater mussels, e.g. the swan mussel, *Arodonta cygnea* and other *Unioidae* on which it relies for reproduction.

It is not native to the British Isles but has been introduced as an ornamental for fish ponds and aquaria, and has gone wild in one or two places, notably around Liverpool and near Northwich in Cheshire. On the Continent it is found from eastern France to western Russia, and south to northern Turkey and the coasts of the Black Sea.

Breeding and growth

The bitterling is unique among European fish in that it depends on freshwater mussels for its reproduction. At spawning time from May to July the female develops a long tube from its anus, the ovipositor, through which it lays its eggs inside the mussel. The male releases its sperm into the water near the mussel, to be sucked in as it inhales. Several eggs are laid in each mussel. The male then guards an area around the mussel against intruders. The eggs hatch in about three weeks and the young fry leave the mussel when their yolk sacs have disappeared.

The bitterling, in return, often acts as host to the parasitic larval stage of the mussel.

The usual size of adult bitterling is 5–8 cm (2–3 in), but exceptional specimens may reach 10 cm (4 in).

Feeding

The diet of bitterling consists mainly of small insect larvae, worms etc., with some plant matter, especially algae.

Its name in German, and in Latin, *amarus*, indicates that the flesh of the bitterling is bitter, but we have not yet had an opportunity to test this.

Characteristics

Dorsal fin: 9–10 rays.
Anal fin: 10–11 rays.
Scales in the lateral line: 30–40.
Pharyngeal teeth: 5 in one row.

Bitterling, young fish, on leaves of plane tree. Photographed 1 December.

Weedy lake near Montélimar, Rhône valley, France.

American catfish from Rhône valley, France. Photographed 20 May.

111

Pumpkinseed from pond near Aubenas, France. Photographed 18 May.

Pumpkinseed

Pumpkinseed. *Lepomis gibbosus* Linn. Family *Centrarchidae*. French,
perche-soleil; German, Sonnenbarsch; Dutch, zonnebaars; Italian,
persico sole.

Recognition and related species
The pumpkinseed is unlikely to be confused with any other fish found
wild in northern Europe. It is small, perch-like, and very deep, but
beautifully coloured with a large dark spot on its gill covers. The two
dorsal fins are joined – the first has nine spiny rays, the second ten soft
rays. Three other small North American bass are given in Maitland's
Guide to the Freshwater Fishes of Britain and Europe. The rock bass
(*Ambloplites rupestris*), said to be established in southern England, has
an indistinct spot on the gill cover and is yellowish brown with darker
markings: it is usually 15–20 cm (6–8 in) long. The other two species are
brighter and smaller. The redbrest sunfish (*Lepomis auritus*) is very
similar to the pumpkinseed, but has its extended opercular flap
completely black. It is recorded from central Italy. The green sunfish
(*L. cyanellus*), however, is less brightly coloured, lacks the red breast,
and is generally golden or greenish with an emerald sheen. It is known in
West Germany.

Habitat and distribution
In Europe, the pumpkinseed is found in weedy lakes and small gravel
pits, usually where the water is well sheltered. In England this species
breeds in a few places, notably near Crawley where we caught young fry
in autumn 1983, in Highgate Pond, and in Somerset near Bridgwater,
but it does better in countries with warmer summers. In southern
France it is common, and it extends northwards into southern Russia
and the Baltic States and eastwards to the mouths of the Danube. It is
said to have been distributed unintentionally with carp fry.

Breeding and growth
Like the other sunfishes (*Centrarchidae*) the pumpkinseed spawns in
early summer, when the water temperature is high (May to August in
England). The male hollows out a nest in shallow water where the
bottom is sandy, often near a log or patch of weed, and defends a
territory round it. After a ritual courtship display the female lays her
eggs in the nest, and they are then fanned and guarded by the male until
they hatch, (in three to five days). The young remain in the nest for
some time further, still guarded by the male, and he continues to protect
them for a few days after they leave the nest. The adults then return to
deeper water, the fry staying in the shallows and remaining in a shoal.
The young mature after two or three years and may live for eight to nine
years. 10–15 cm (4–6 in) is the usual adult size, but 22 cm (8½ in)
specimens weighing 330 gm (12 oz) have been recorded.

Feeding
Pumpkinseed eat mainly small crustaceans and insect larvae.

Fishing for pumpkinseed
Small hooks and delicate tackle are all that are needed to catch this little
fish, and a small active worm is a suitable bait. They fight like small
devils.
When the males are defending their nests they will attack anything
which goes near, so something imitating a small stickleback might make
an effective lure. Summer is the best time, for then the fish are near the
edge and can often be seen sunning themselves, lying quite still near the
surface.
The pumpkinseed is very good to eat but bony. The tiny specimens
found in England are unlikely to be edible, but in America where it
grows large it is regularly eaten.

Characteristics
Dorsal fin: 10 (or 11) spines and 10 rays.
Anal fin: 3 spines and 10–11 rays.
Scales along the lateral line: 35–47.

Buchan Park Lake, near Crawley, Sussex.

Lake near Montélimar, Rhône valley, France.

Largemouth bass

Largemouth bass. *Micropterus salmoides* Lacepede. Family
Centrarchidae. French, black bass; German, Forellenbarsch; Dutch,
zwarte baars.

Recognition and related species

A largemouth bass is like a large perch, though without red fins and with
less distinct bars. Its back is primarily green, with irregular blotches as
bars all along the middle line. The first dorsal has nine spiny rays and is
slightly smaller than the soft-rayed second dorsal.
This species, and the smallmouth bass (*M. dolomieui*) are collectively
known as black bass. The small-mouth has a smaller mouth, and smaller
scales, 68–78 in the lateral line. It is usually yellower in colour, and less
heavily barred, and its two dorsal fins are joined.

Habitat and distribution

Largemouth bass are found in bays in lakes, in ponds and more rarely in
rivers. They remain near the surface, and usually near weed beds or
other vegetation. They are native of North America from the Great
Lakes to the Mississippi, but have been widely spread as a game fish.
England has not proved to be a suitable area for them, though there is
said to have been a colony in a lake east of Wareham in Dorset since
1934. Most of the country is too cold in summer, as bass prefer a water
temperature of 20–24°C (68–75°F) only reached in sheltered ponds in
hot summers. They have, however, been established successfully on the
Continent, especially in France, Germany and Poland. In some places,
e.g. the Rhône valley, they have been introduced in an effort to control
large populations of small American catfish (p.110).

Breeding and growth

Spawning takes place between March and July, in a depression in the
sandy bottom of the lake. The male actively guards the eggs and the
young fry, attacking anything that comes near, including other males
and females. While involved in these duties, he eats little.
The young mature after three to four years and reach 20–50 cm
(8–20 in) when adult. Maximum size is 82 cm (30 in) and weight of
10 kg (22¼ lb).

Feeding

Largemouth bass are active predators, eating crustaceans and other
invertebrates when young, mainly fish when larger. Their general
behaviour seems to be similar to that of perch in Europe, though they
grow much larger.

Fishing for bass

Black bass are two of the most popular sport species in North America.
They are fished with plugs, spinners and large worms. One very
effective method, in daytime, is to use leaded streamer flies made of
bucktail and jerk them upwards from the bottom in imitation of small
fish. Minnows and tadpoles are favourite bass food and make good baits.

Cooking bass

Black bass are good eating. American Indians made a soup of them with
wild rice.

Characteristics

1st dorsal fin: 9 spiny rays. 2nd dorsal fin: 12 rays.
Scales along the lateral line: 60–68.

Largemouth bass from Brown Co. State Park, Indiana. Photographed 5 August.

River Coln, Middlesex.

Three-spined stickleback

Three-spined stickleback. *Gasterosteus aculeatus* Linn. Family
Gasterosteidae. French, epinoch; German, Stichling; Swedish,
storspigg; Dutch, stekelbaars.

Recognition and related species

The three-spined stickleback is the smallest of British freshwater fish,
seldom exceeding 7 cm (3 in) in length. It is easily recognized by the
three large spines on its back, the well-developed pectoral fins, and the
ventral fins reduced to spines. Basically the fish is silvery with a greenish
back, but the males, particularly in spring, have vivid red underparts.
The only closely related species in fresh water is Europe is the ten- (or
nine-) spined stickleback which is easily distinguished by having eight to
ten shorter spines on its back, and being darker in colour; the male with
a black throat in the breeding season.

The three-spined stickleback occurs in Britain in three forms, which
differ in the presence and number of bony plates which take the place of
scales in this fish. These forms are called *leiurus*, smooth without bony
plates, *semiarmatus*, with a few bony plates, and *trachurus*, with a
complete row of plates from just in front of the pectoral fins to the tail.

Habitat and distribution

In Britain the three-spined stickleback is found in all waters from tiny
streams to shallow places in rivers, estuaries and the sea, though
normally close to the coast around low tide mark. The three forms differ
somewhat in their ecology; *leiurus* spend all their time in fresh water,
and are the usual form inland; *semiarmatus* and *trachurus* spend most of
the winter in the sea, and enter fresh water in spring to breed.
Recently, during a survey in 1980, very large numbers of sticklebacks
were found in the South Forty Foot near Boston, the population
increasing towards the sea. 63% of these were found to be *trachurus*; 31%
semiarmatus, and only 6% *leiurus* suggesting that this is a largely
migratory population, which had entered fresh water to breed.
Three-spined sticklebacks are found throughout the British Isles, but
are commonest in the south and east of England, and apparently rare in
Scotland and Ireland. On the Continent they are mainly coastal, and are
found along the Atlantic and Mediterranean coasts as far east as Albania,
and around the coast of the Black Sea. They are also found in South
Iceland, the north-east USA, and Canada, and around the North
Pacific, mainly in coastal areas.

Breeding and growth

Sticklebacks breed in spring and early summer; the male makes a nest of
vegetable fibres on the bottom, having first driven off any other males
which may try to establish a territory nearby. He then sets out to attract a

Three-spined sticklebacks from river Chess, Bucks. Photographed 2 August.

suitably ripe female, and the two indulge in a strictly ritualized courtship
display. The male dances backwards and forwards in a zig-zag, and the
female, if she is ready to spawn, follows. If any false step is made, the
courtship fails. The male leads the female to his nest, she darts in and
lays a few eggs, which are immediately fertilized. The female then goes
off, the male remains to guard the nest and next day attracts another
female to lay her quota. The male continues to watch over the nest until
the young, usually from 60 to 120 in number, hatch and catches food for
them for the first two weeks or so, until they can fend for themselves.

Feeding

Sticklebacks are largely carnivorous, eating small crustaceans, larvae,
small fish or worms. They also eat a certain amount of plant material.

Fishing for sticklebacks

Sticklebacks are the usual tiddlers caught by children in nets; suitable
prey as they are usually found in shallow water. An easier way of

Lake Mustaselkä, Finland.

catching them is on a worm tied in the middle with cotton. The greedy fish will attack the worm and swallow the head or tail, hanging on so keenly that they can be lifted gently out of the water and dropped into a jam jar, sometimes two at a time; the worm can then be replaced.

Characteristics
1st dorsal fin: 3 spines without membrane.
2nd dorsal fin: 10–12 rays. Anal fin: 1 spine, 8–9 rays.
Scales absent, but sometimes replaced by scale-like bony plates.

Ten-spined stickleback
Ten-spined stickleback. *Pungitius pungitius* Linn. French, epinochette; German, Zwergstickling; Swedish, smaspigg; Dutch, tiendoornige stekelbaars; Finnish, kynnenpiikki.

Recognition and related species
The ten-spined stickleback is distinguished from the more common three-spined by its darker colour and by the ten (eight to ten) short (as opposed to three longer) spines along its back. The spines are modified first dorsal fin rays, and the ventral fins are also modified into spines. There is one closely related stickleback in fresh water in Europe, the Ukranian stickleback *P. Platygaster*. It also has ten spines, but does not have the lateral keel on the caudal peduncle. Another species, a fifteen-spined stickleback, (*Spinachia spinachia*) is entirely marine. It is much slenderer than either of the other species.

Habitat and distribution
Ten-spined sticklebacks are usually found in stiller waters than three-spined. They are common in small very weedy ponds, and though found in brackish water, are seldom found in the sea proper.
In England, the ten-spined stickleback is less common than the three-spined, and is found mainly in the east and in the Midlands. It appears to be rare in Scotland and the southwest of England. In Ireland it is widespread, especially in the central plain, around Lough Neagh, and in the far south.
On the Continent, the ten-spined stickleback is found only in the north and near the coast from Holland eastwards to the Baltic.

Breeding and growth
In general the breeding habits are similar to those of the three-spined. The male usually builds the nest some way off the bottom, though occasionally (in the American Great Lakes) on the bottom or in a burrow. The nests are usually in weed beds whereas those of the three-spined are in more open areas.

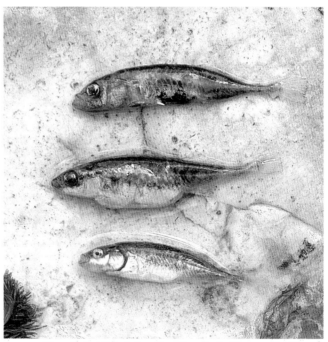

Ten-spined sticklebacks from river Chess, Bucks. Photographed 2 August.

The males remain black in the breeding season and do not develop red underparts.
The young are adult by the end of their first summer and usually do not live more than three years; their length is 3–5 cm (1½–2 in).

Feeding
Small crustacea such as *Daphnia* are probably the main food of ten-spined sticklebacks, though they will probably eat any invertebrates of a suitable size, as well as small fish.
The same methods as are used for catching three-spined sticklebacks can be successful with ten-spined. Because they can tolerate lower oxygen levels, they are easier to keep in a fish tank, where they should be provided with plenty of weed such as *Elodea*, for cover.

Characteristics
1st dorsal fin: 10 (sometimes 8 or 9) separate short spines.
2nd dorsal fin: 9–10 rays.

Lake Jaminginselkä, Finland.

Burbot

Burbot or eel pout. *Lota lota* Linn. Family *Gadidae*. French, lote de rivière; German, Quappe; Swedish, lake; Dutch, kwabaal; Finnish, made.

Recognition and related species

This is the only European member of the cod family to live in fresh water. It is an elongated fish with a short first dorsal and very long second dorsal and anal fins. It has one well developed chin barbel, and long, soft modified ventral fins equipped with taste buds. The most similar species are the rocklings and the ling which are exclusively marine. The rocklings all have the first dorsal reduced to a single spine and a narrow fringe of rays. The ling are even more slender with fewer rays in their second dorsal and anal fins. The only freshwater fish with which the burbot might be confused is the wels or catfish (p.108) but this can be distinguished at a glance by its one very small dorsal fin. The old name, eel pout, is very appropriate for this fish as it is smooth and slimy to handle, curling its tail round anything as does an eel.

Habitat and distribution

The burbot is found in the lower reaches of sluggish rivers, in lakes and in brackish parts of the Baltic. In colder water it lives in association with trout and bullhead, in warmer places with other coarse fish. It is nocturnal, living in deep holes, under stones or in weed or other cover during the day, and emerging to feed, being most active in the evening or at dawn, and in cold water, below 7°C (44°F). The burbot is possibly now extinct in the British Isles. Formerly they were common in some of the fenland rivers and drains. Indeed Mascall in the *Booke of Fishing with Hooke and Line* (1590) says, 'They have such a plentie in the fenne brookes, they feed their hogges with them.' They were also frequent in the Trent and its tributaries. The last recorded capture of a burbot, as far as we have been able to discover, was on the old West River, a tributary of the Great Ouse, near Cambridge, but none have been seen for about twelve years. On the Continent, burbot are found from central France (including the Rhône basin) eastwards across central Europe and Siberia to the Pacific and across the whole of North America. They extend far to the north into Arctic Europe, Siberia, Alaska and Canada.

Breeding and growth

Burbot spawn in the middle of winter, in December and January, laying huge numbers of minute eggs, possibly five million in a large female, over stones and gravel, under the ice. At this period the fish congregate in large numbers, and the burbot is one of the species regularly caught by fishing through holes in the ice.

Growth is rather slow, the young maturing after three or four years. Average size is 30–50 cm (12–20 in), and a weight of about 1 kg (2 lb) – the maximum size recorded in Europe is 120 cm (48 in), 32 kg (72 lb).

Feeding

Burbot are mainly carnivorous, eating small fish of all sorts, and other aquatic animals, such as crayfish and insect larvae. They feed in daytime in deeper water, and move into the shallows at night.

Fishing for burbot

Because of its sedentary habits, its mainly nocturnal feeding and sluggish movements, the burbot is not a favoured game fish.

It can, however, be caught in winter through holes in the ice and is otherwise best taken by night lines baited with a bunch of large worms, or a small fish, such as a trout, perch, ruffe or bream. It is said to be especially active before storms or during high water after rain.

Cooking burbot

Burbot flesh is excellent, firm, white and very tasty, similar to that of the monkfish (French lotte). The liver is very oily, like that of its relative, the cod. They are said to be in better condition for eating in winter, but some which we tried in June, grilled over an open fire, were very good.

Characteristics

1st dorsal fin: 14 rays. 2nd dorsal fin: 68 rays. Anal fin: 67 rays.
Ventral fins modified into soft feelers. One chin barbel.
Scales small, embedded in the skin.

Burbot from Lake Jäminginselkä. Photographed 27 June.

Spined loach from Fodder dyke near Boston, Lincolnshire with water-milfoil and green algae.

Spined loach

Spined loach. *Cobitis taenia* Linn. Family *Cobitidae*. French, loche de rivière; German, Steinbeisser; Swedish, nissoga; Dutch, kleine modderkruiper.

Recognition and related species

The spined loach can best be distinguished from the more familiar stone loach (p.48) by the two rows of dark spots along its body and by its laterally flattened body, giving it the profile, in cross-section, of a Turkish cigarette. Its tail is rounded at the end and it has six short equal barbels around its mouth. The name spined loach refers to a moveable double spine below each eye, not found in the stone loach, but not easily seen on living specimens.

The only other common loach in Europe is the weather loach, *Misgurnus fossilis*. It inhabits rich ponds, lakes and other stagnant water, from Holland eastwards. It is distinguished by having ten barbels around its mouth, and a sandy-coloured body with dark stripes running from head to tail.

Habitat and distribution

In contrast to the stone loach, the spined loach is found in the lower reaches of slow rivers, canals and ditches in company with roach, pike, dace, bleak and gudgeon. It lives on the bottom, often half hidden in fine sand or mud.

In the British Isles, spined loach are not common. They are absent from Ireland and Scotland, and in England are found only in the east, mainly in Lincolnshire, in the rivers running into the Wash and in the upper reaches of the Thames.

On the Continent, the spined loach is widespread from Spain and North Africa eastwards to Siberia, China and Japan, south to Italy and Turkey and north to southern Sweden.

Breeding and growth

Spawning takes place between April and June, when the eggs are attached to weeds, mainly algae, in shallow water.

Normal size is 7–10 cm (3–4 in), with a maximum of 14 cm (5½ in).

Feeding

Mainly worms, insect larvae and small crustaceans.

Fishing for spined loach

The spined loach is not often seen by anglers, but is sometimes caught during the electric fishing surveys carried out by water authorities or fishery scientists. Even so they are seldom caught as most of the nets used in fishery sampling are of too large mesh to take them.

Characteristics

Dorsal fin: 10 rays.
Anal fin: 7 rays.
Pectoral fin: 6–9 rays.
Barbels: 6 short, equal.

Dyke near Boston, Lincolnshire.

Elvers from Severn Estuary. Photographed 8 May.

Eel

Eel. *Anguilla anguilla* Linn. Family *Anguillidae*. French, anguille; German, Aal; Swedish, oal; Dutch, aal or paling; Finnish, ankerias.

Recognition and related species

The eel is the commonest snake-like fish; it has a normal fish-like mouth and eyes, small gills and pectoral fins, and a narrow dorsal fin which is united to the caudal and anal fins, the three forming a parallel fringe all round the posterior half of the eel. Lampreys have sucker-like mouths and even more reduced fins. There are no related species in fresh water, but there are two rather similar marine eels, the conger and the moray. The conger has the dorsal fin starting well forward near the pectoral fins and can grow large, up to 3 m (9 ft) long. The moray is a more southern fish, rare around Britain and easily distinguished by having no pectoral fins and small slits for gills.

Habitat and distribution

Eels are found in all types of fresh water, from clear rocky rivers to muddy ditches and ponds. They usually live on the bottom, and over-winter hidden in the mud.

Eels are found in fresh water throughout Europe from northern Norway and Sweden southwards, eastwards to the Black Sea, and around the Mediterranean to the Canary Islands. A very similar species, *A. rostrata*, is found on the Atlantic coast of North America.

Breeding and growth

Eels spawn in the Atlantic Ocean, somewhere to the south-east of Bermuda, in an area known as the Sargasso Sea. Spawning eels have never been captured, but the young larvae have been found in the plankton in the Sargasso Sea area at 90–270 m (300–900 ft) depth, so it is assumed that spawning takes place there, probably at even greater depth. At an age of about two months the larvae are about 2.5 cm (1 in) long, narrowly ovate and leaf-like with a minute head. They drift towards Europe on the Gulf Stream, growing slowly, until at a length of about 6.5 cm (2¾ in) and age of 2½ years, they reach the coast of Europe. At this stage they still look very un-eel-like, and were once thought to be a distinct fish called *Leptocephalus*. They metamorphose into elvers in the sea, and millions of them, at this stage about 7 cm (2⅘ in) long, move into fresh water in May and June swimming in shallow water up the rivers and even over wet rocks at the edge of waterfalls and other barriers.

Eels have the capacity to survive out of water much longer than most fish and are known to travel across land through wet grass. They are enabled to do this by closing their small gills, and keeping them supplied with water held in a large gill cavity. These can be seen as swellings on either side of the head when the eel is out of water.

It is not known exactly how long eels remain in fresh water (one is recorded to have lived in the Jardin des Plantes in Paris for thirty-seven years, fed on beef), nor is it known by what stimulus they become sexually mature and return to the sea to spawn. As it nears the sea, its body colour changes from golden to silvery and its eye increases in size, adapting it to life in the ocean depths.

Mature eels vary greatly in size. Males are usually smaller, up to 50 cm (20 in), females up to 100 cm (40 in). Specimens up to 14 kg (28 lb) are recorded, but 1.5 kg (3 lb) is a common maximum size. The British rod-caught record at present stands at 5.05 kg (11 lb 2 oz) from a lake in Hampshire, caught by S. Terry in 1978.

Feeding

Eels are primarily scavengers, but will take all kinds of live food including young fish, birds, etc. They are particularly damaging to the spawn of salmon and trout which are laid in gravel.

Fishing for eels

Most anglers will have caught eels at some time in their lives, probably when fishing with a worm for other species. They usually swallow the hook and make a frightful mess of the line – and the angler – with their combination of wriggling and slime.

For catching large eels, a whole fish dead bait is recommended, something such as a 12.5 cm (5 in) roach. It should be fished on the bottom, so it is important that its swim bladder be punctured so that it sinks. A soluble bag containing smelly groundbait and a stone to act as extra weight for casting can be put on to the line so that the eels are attracted into the area of the bait. It is important that the line be unweighted and left free to run out so that the eel does not feel any resistance when it first picks up the bait, and so drop it before it is hooked. Other baits which are recommended are fish liver, pieces of kipper, crayfish or prawns. With the whole fish bait the strike should be made when the eel makes its second run with the bait, but with the other baits striking can be as soon as the line moves out.

Eels make excellent eating; jellied eels are a traditional favourite in the East End of London; but smoked eel has a more universal appeal. The flesh is rich, firm, and excellent in flavour. Elvers, when they first move out of the sea, are also caught in large numbers. Most are now sent to eel farms, but along the Severn estuary they are still eaten fried, especially in the form of elver cakes, which have 'a peculiar appearance from the number of little black eyes that bespangle them'. We found them excellent when deep fried with a little garlic.

Characteristics

Dorsal, caudal (tail) and anal fins continuous, narrow.
Scales minute, embedded in the skin.

Eel from river Test, Hampshire. Photographed 6 October.

Vimba (*not illustrated*)

Vimba. *Vimba vimba* Linn. Family *Cyprinidae*. German, Zahrte;
Swedish, vimma; Finnish, vimpa; Austrian, Russnase.

Recognition and related species

Many fish of different families or in different groups in the carp family
(*Cyprinidae*) have inferior mouths and elongated upper jaws forming a
snout. The vimba is one of these; its mouth is similar to that of the nase
(p.66), its snout is even more elongated. Its long anal fin, however, with
18–21 branched rays, indicates its relationship with the bream, but it is
distinctly less deep than the species of bream. It differs from the bream
also in having a scaled keel behind the dorsal fin. Its colour is generally
silvery with a dark back, but in the breeding season the males become
black above, and deep orange beneath the head, belly and lower fins.

Habitat and distribution

The vimba is found in both large slow rivers and brackish seas where it
lives and feeds on the bottom.

It is common in parts of eastern Europe, in Poland, e.g. the river Vistula,
and parts of the Baltic, and in the rivers entering the Black and Caspian
seas. It is also recorded from southern Sweden and northern Germany.

Breeding and growth

Before spawning vimba make an upstream migration which may be as
long as 560 km (350 miles). The spawning fish gather in shoals and lay
their eggs over a clean stony bottom or on weeds in shallow running
water. The adult size of 20–30 cm (8–12 in) and 490 gm (1 lb), is
reached in six to eight years. Maximum size is 50 cm (20 in) and a weight
of about 3 kg (6½ lb).

Feeding

Vimba are bottom feeders, as is suggested by their mouth position, and
live on worms, insect larvae and molluscs.

Fishing for vimba

Boiled barley is recommended as a good bait for vimba, though bread
paste, pieces of worms and maggots may also be successful. The bait
should be fished with a float so it swims just above the bottom.

Characteristics

Dorsal fin: 10 rays. Anal fin: 18–21 rays.
Scales along the lateral line: 57–63. Pharyngeal teeth: 5 in one row.

Chekhon (*not illustrated*)

Chekhon, ziege. *Pelecus cultratus* Linn. Family *Cyprinidae*. German,
Ziege; Swedish, stärkniv; Finnish, miekkasärki; Russian, chekhon.

Recognition and related species

The chekhon is one of the most distinctive members of the carp family.
Its mouth is strongly superior, the well-developed lower jaw curving
upwards to meet the shortened upper jaw. The pectoral fins are
well-developed, long and pointed. The dorsal fin is small and set far back
on the body, almost opposite the very long-based anal fin.

In colour it is silvery, with a bluish-green sheen on its nearly straight
back, and pinkish on the sides. The belly is deep and strongly curved,
the lateral line is wavy, running along the lower part of the body.

Habitat and distribution

The chekhon is found only in the lower reaches of rivers, in dams, in
estuaries and in brackish seas. In the sea it swims in shoals in open water,
in rivers it lives in the stiller deep water on bends.

It is restricted to the southern Baltic, the northern parts of the Black and
Caspian seas, to the Aral Sea, and to the lower reaches of the rivers
which enter them, such as the Danube, the Volga, the Don and the
Oxus. It is also found in parts of Denmark and southern Sweden.

The Baltic sea, near Pargas, Finland, habitat of some fish we couldn't catch.

Breeding and growth

Chekhon breed in fresh or brackish water, and, at least in the south of their range, run some way up rivers. Spawning takes place on weed and other vegetation from May to July. The young remain in rivers or estuaries for their first few years before migrating to the sea, and mature after three to four years.

Average size is 25–40 cm (10–15 in) and a weight of about 500 gm (1 lb). Maximum recorded weight is 3.5 kg (7¾ lb), though most do not exceed 1.5 kg (3¼ lb).

Feeding

As is indicated by the position of its mouth, the chekhon feeds primarily on the surface, on young fish such as herrings and cod in the Baltic, and in other areas on other species. In fresh water they also eat surface insects and small crustaceans.

Fishing for chekhon

In eastern Europe the chekhon forms the basis of a minor commercial fishery. It is usually eaten salted or smoked.

Characteristics

Dorsal fin: 7 rays. Anal fin: 24–28 rays.
Scales along the lateral line: 90–115.

Sturgeon (*not illustrated*)

Sturgeon. *Acipenser sturio* Linn. Family *Acipenseridae*. French, esturgeon; German, Stor; Swedish, stor; Dutch, steur; Finnish, sampi.

Recognition and related species

Sturgeon are instantly recognizable by their huge size and elongated body with rows of bony plates along the side and back. The tail is also peculiar, with the backbone turning up into the upper lobe.

In colour the sturgeon is greenish-brown to black on the back, paler and yellowish beneath. There are no other species in western Europe, but others such as the Beluga (*Huso huso* Linn.) and the Sevrjuga (*A. stellatus* Pallas), known for their caviare, are found in the Danube and the northern Adriatic.

Habitat and distribution

In the British Isles sturgeon are now mere vagrants, occasionally landed by fishing boats. During the last century, individuals were caught in the Conway river, just below Tal-y-Cafn bridge, and in the Wye at Chepstow and in one or two other estuaries. On the Continent they are also very rare, and only now spawn in the Gironde and the Guadelquivir.

Breeding and growth

Spawning takes place in deep water in rivers, the eggs being shed on to gravel to which they stick. The young stay in fresh water for about three years before migrating to the sea where they live for eight to fifteen years before returning to spawn, usually in early summer.

Specimens caught in England weighed between 320 and 450 lb, but the largest recorded was about 3.5 m (11½ ft) long and weighed 320 kg (700 lb).

Feeding

Young sturgeon in rivers eat bottom-living larvae, crustaceans and molluscs.

Fishing for sturgeon

Because of the excellence of their flesh, said to taste 'like a compound of veal and eel, with a flavouring of lobster', and the value of their roe for making caviare, sturgeon have always been much sought after.

Twaite shad

Twaite shad. *Alosa fallax* Lacépède. Family *Clupeidae*. French, alose feinte; German, Finte; Swedish, staksill; Dutch, fint.

Recognition and related species
The shads are members of the herring family, and so related also to sprats and pilchards. They are primarily estuarine or coastal fish, entering fresh water only to spawn.

Shads are easily recognized by their plump-looking silvery bodies with large loose scales, small fins, and tails with two pointed areas of scales reaching almost to the fork. Most species also have a dark spot on the body near the upper edge of the gill cover. The west European species belong to the genus *Alosa*, the species in the Black and Caspian seas to *Caspialosa*. The two genera differ mainly in the presence or absence of vomerine teeth, absent in *Alosa*, present in *Caspialosa*.

Two species of shad are found in the British Isles. The twaite is now much the commoner. It has less than 70 scales in the lateral line, and 40–60 gill rakers. The allis shad (*Alosa alosa*) is now much rarer; it has more than 70 scales in the lateral line, and 80–130 gill rakers. The irregular spots along the back of the twaite are not apparent when the fish is fresh, but appear as it dries. The allis shad does not have more than one spot at the shoulder.

Habitat and distribution
The twaite shad is found all round the coasts of the British Isles, from Norway and the western Baltic southwards to North Africa, and throughout the Mediterranean. Totally freshwater populations are found in some large lakes, notably in the Killarney Lakes in south-west Ireland, and in Lakes Lugano, Como and Maggiore in the southern Alps. In England the largest population is found in the Severn, and many are taken in the estuary in putches (traps) intended for salmon. Occasional specimens are caught by sea anglers around the coasts.

Breeding and growth
The twaite shad spawns in fresh water in the lower reaches of rivers, normally still within the influence of the tide. The main run is in April and May, and spawning takes place in May and June. In the Rhône, the Mediterranean subspecies was formerly found as far upriver as Lyon, but now its passage upstream is prevented by numerous barrages. Adults mature at three to four years, by which time they are around 30 cm (1 ft) long and weigh about 0.73 kg (1 lb 10 oz). Exceptionally they may be 55 cm (22 in) long and weigh 1.5 kg (3 lb 5 oz).

Feeding
Twaite shad feed mainly on small planktonic crustaceans, but also take fry of other species. They are said not to feed during their spawning migrations, and indeed the one specimen we examined, a female full of roe, had nothing in its gut.

Fishing for shad
As already mentioned, most shad are caught in putches, funnel-shaped baskets set in the channel of the tidal Severn. Most of the putches are positioned to catch fish moving downstream on the ebb tide, because the fish tend to keep to the middle of the river when moving upstream on the flood, and descend near the bank.

Shads can also be caught by angling, either by spinning with a small spoon, or by fly fishing, using nymphs or small streamer flies.

Cooking shad
The twaite shad is usually considered inferior to the allis shad. Both are like large herrings with rich flesh, but marred by being very bony: they are cooked in similar ways.

The shads caught on the Severn in Gloucestershire were formerly sold to the mining villages in the Forest of Dean, but nowadays they are discarded as a nuisance when caught in the traps designed for salmon. In France, shads are a speciality of the Loire in spring and cooked in a variety of ways, often accompanied by a sauce of sorrel. Jane Grigson recommends softening the bones by very slow cooking for six hours encased in foil and a fish so treated is very tasty, the bones being reduced to a crunchy consistency similar to those of a tinned sardine.

For those who do not want to bother with long cooking, but have access to a good supply of shads, the roes, both hard and soft, are excellent when fried quickly in butter.

Severn estuary near Lydney, Gloucestershire.

Characteristics
Dorsal fin: 19–21 rays.
Anal fin: 20–24 rays.
Scales in the lateral line: less than 70.

Allis shad (*not illustrated*)

Allis shad. *Alosa alosa* Linn. Family *Clupeidae*. French, grande alose; German, Maifisch; Dutch, elft; Norwegian, maisild.

Recognition and related species
The allis shad is very similar to the twaite shad in general appearance and habits; the anatomical differences between the two are mentioned under the twaite.

The allis shad is now very rare and the only breeding population in the British Isles is probably in southern Ireland. Only a few specimens are caught each year in the Severn, but it was formerly found regularly as far north as the Tay, where a few are still caught each year. It spawns higher up river than the twaite, well into fresh water in running water, and this is one possible reason for its decline. On the Continent the allis shad has a similar distribution to the twaite, but it does not extend into the Baltic, and is found only in the western Mediterranean. The allis shad is usually somewhat larger than the twaite reaching a maximum of 70 cm (28 in) and a weight of 2.75 kg (6 lb), though a weight of 1.37 kg (3 lb) is usual.

Characteristics
Dorsal fin: 19–21 rays.
Anal fin: 20–24 rays.
Scales in the lateral line: more than 70.

Twaite shad from Severn estuary. Photographed 4 May.

Pipefish (S. rostellatus) *from Thames estuary. Photographed 26 October.*

Pipefish

Pipefish. *Syngnathus rostellatus*, *S. typhle*, *S. acus* and *Nerophis ophidion*. Family *Syngnathidae*. French, syngnathe.

Recognition and related species

Pipefish are very slender and delicate-looking, but surprisingly tough and wiry in the hand. They are easily recognized by their slender bodies, with only the dorsal fin at all developed, big eyes and snout-like mouths. The four species listed above are the commonest in estuarine waters of the six species found in northern Europe. They differ fom one another in several ways. *N. ophidion* is the most distinct, having 28–32 segments in front of the very narrow dorsal fin and a thin pointed tail. The *Syngnathus* species have about 17 segments in front of a larger dorsal fin and a small rounded fin at the end of the tail. *S. acus* has a long tubular snout, *S. typhle* has a laterally flattened snout and *S. rostellatus* (illustrated) a short tubular snout.
Another species, *S. abaster* is found along the coast of the northern Mediterranean.
This family also contains two *Hippocampus* species, the familiar sea horses, which are common in the Mediterranean but rare in northern waters.

Habitat and distribution

Pipefish usually live among seaweeds, particularly eel grass (*Zostera*), in shallow water. *S. rostellatus* is said by Alwyne Wheeler to be especially abundant in estuaries, and the specimens photographed here were caught in the Thames estuary near Tilbury.
All species are found all round the coasts of Britain. *S. rostellatus* is found only in northwest Europe, and is absent from the Baltic. *S. acus* is also absent from the Baltic, but common in the Mediterranean. *S. typhle* and *N. ophidion* are both found in the southern Baltic, south to the whole of the Mediterranean and the Black Sea.

Breeding and growth

Spawning takes place in May and June, when the fish migrate into deeper water. In *Syngnathus* the eggs are laid by the female in a pouch made by folds of skin along the body of the male who broods them until they hatch. In *Nerophis* the eggs are simply attached to the concave belly of the male. *S. acus* is the largest species, reaching a maximum of 47 cm (19 in). *S. rostellatus* reaches only 17 cm (7 in) and *S. typhle* 30 cm (1 ft).

Feeding

Pipefish feed on small planktonic crustaceans and very small fish.

Tub Gurnard

Tub gurnard, tubfish, yellow or blue gurnard, gurnet. *Trigla lucerna* Linn. Family *Triglidae*. French, trigle or gurnard.

Recognition and related species

Gurnards are easily recognized by their large angular heads and tapering bodies, and by having the lower three rays of the pectoral fins separate, thickened and feeler-like.
Gurnards also have the unusual attribute of being able to communicate by sound. Their grunt-like snores are made by special muscles attached to the swim bladder.
The tub gurnard is recognized by its well-developed pectoral fins which are bright blue, edged with red. In the other species these fins are neither so well developed nor brightly coloured. The red gurnard is distinguished by its dark red body and the row of scales along its side. The third common species in British waters is the grey gurnard, which has shorter pectoral fins, and a greyish body with pale spots; a dark patch on its first pectoral fin is also characteristic.

Habitat and distribution

The tub gurnard is characteristic of muddy or sandy bottoms in shallow water, usually in the sea, but it is also found in estuaries such as the Thames, where it is common. It is a widespread species in the western Atlantic, occurring all along the coast from central Norway to North Africa, and all around the Mediterranean.

Red gurnard (above) *and tub gurnard* (below) *from the Thames estuary. Photographed 26 October.*

Breeding and growth
Tub gurnard spawn in open sea in late summer and autumn. Adult length is around 50–60 cm (20–24 in), though specimens up to 75 cm (30 in), weighing 5.5 kg (12 lb 3 oz) have been recorded. Other large specimens from 3.4–4.5 kg (8–10 lb) have been caught off the west of Ireland.

Feeding
Tub gurnard feed on the bottom, living on crustaceans, crabs, and small fish. They hunt by swimming near the seabed, probing in the mud for prey with their feelers.

Characteristics
1st dorsal fin: 8–9 spines. 2nd dorsal fin: 16 spiny rays.
Anal fin: 15–16 rays.

Red Gurnard
Aspitrigla cuculus Day. Family *Triglidae*.

Recognition and related species
The red gurnard differs from the tub mainly in its smaller size, deeper red colour and shorter pectorals. Other differences are mentioned under the tub gurnard.

Habitat and distribution
The red gurnard is found in shallow water, usually on sand or gravel, but sometimes among rocks. It is less widespread than the tub, being found only as far north as Denmark and western Scotland, and being absent from the eastern-most Mediterranean.

Breeding and growth
Spawning takes place in summer. Normal adult length is around 40 cm (16 in) and a maximum of 1 kg (2 lb). The British record was 2.26 kg (5 lb), caught by D. B. Critchley (aged nine) off Rhyl.

Feeding
Mainly crabs and crustaceans, but also small fish and other bottom-living animals.

Fishing for gurnards
Gurnards are commonly caught by anglers, a most favourable mark being near rocks surrounded by sand. Recommended baits are worms or pieces of fish (salted mackerel is especially favoured), but gurnards may also be caught on a baited spoon dragged along the seabed, as is used for flounders. Gurnards usually occur in shoals, so where one has been caught others may be expected.

Characteristics
1st dorsal fin: 8–9 spines. 2nd dorsal fin: 18 spiny rays.
Anal fin: 16–17 rays.

Smelt

Smelt. *Osmerus eperlanus* Linn. Family *Osmeridae*. French, éperlan; German, Stint; Dutch, spiering; Norwegian, krohle.

Recognition and related species

The smelt is a small silvery fish, with a greenish back, and an almost translucent skin. It has an adipose fin like the salmon family, to which it is related, and is distinguished from them, and from the whitefishes, by its short lateral line, which does not extend to behind the pectoral fin, and its relatively large mouth with numerous long sharp teeth. There are no other species of smelt in Europe, but there are other species in the Pacific and there is a closely related fish, the capelin, which is found in huge numbers in the Arctic seas. The smelt is also unusual in smelling strongly of cucumber.

Habitat and distribution

The smelt is usually found in estuaries, from which it migrates upriver in large numbers in winter to spawn in fresh water. It is found all round the coasts of the British Isles where there are suitable silty or sandy and unpolluted estuaries. On the Continent it is found along the coasts from the Bay of Biscay northwards to the Baltic and the White Sea, and in Scandinavia and western Russia. Land-locked populations are common in fresh water, usually in lowland lakes.

Breeding and growth

Spawning takes place in March and April in fresh water around the limit of tidal influence, the eggs being laid over sand or gravel, or on to weeds. At 1½-years-old smelt are 7.5–10 cm (3–4 in) long, and they reach their maximum length of 30 cm (12 in) in about four years.
The British rod-caught record is 191 gm (6 oz 12 drm), caught by G. Idiens at Fleetwood, Lancs in 1961.

Feeding

Smaller fish feed mainly on shrimps and other crustaceans, the larger specimens, which are mostly female, on small fish.

Fishing for smelt

Because of its small size, the smelt has not received much attention from anglers, though it can be caught on light tackle and a small worm. As it is a predatory fish a small fly might also be effective.
Smelt are excellent to eat, being similar to, but more delicate than, a sprat. They were formerly the subject of a very important fishery in the Thames and the Forth, but were driven away by pollution, and have only recently returned in large numbers.

Characteristics

Dorsal fin: 11 rays. Anal fin: 12–16 rays.
Adipose fin present.

Smelts from Thames estuary, West Thurrock. Photographed 26 October.

Estuary of river Coln, Essex.

Brightlingsea reach, Essex.

Flounder

Flounder. *Platichthys flesus* Linn. Family *Pleuronectidae*. French, flet; German, Flunder; Swedish, skrubbskädda; Dutch, bot. Local name: fluke (Ireland).

Recognition and related species
The flounder is a typical flatfish, similar to the better-known plaice (see p.134). Flounders are characterized by having a line of prickles along the bases of both fins, and along the lateral line. The anal fin has 35–46 rays compared with that of the plaice which has 48–59 rays. The eyes and colouring are normally on the right-hand side of the fish, but 'reversed' specimens, with the eyes on the left-hand side are quite common.

Habitat and distribution
Of all the flatfish, the flounder is the only one which is tolerant of fresh water, occurring commonly in harbours and estuaries, and in some places in completely fresh water, though always where there is an easy connection to the sea. Young flounders hatched at sea move into the estuaries in late spring and early summer, riding up on the tide and lying stationary on the bottom on the ebb. Adult flounders move back into the estuaries and rivers after spawning; Herbert Maxwell suggests that they follow the easy food source of the migrating elvers. They are commonest in muddy and sandy estuaries, and are especially frequent on the east coast of England and the low countries. The flounder is one of the most widespread of all the flatfish, occurring from the northernmost parts of Norway and Sweden, throughout the Baltic, and south to the whole coastline of the Mediterranean and Black seas. It lives more in fresh water in the northern part of its range, though we were still surprised to catch one while netting powan in Loch Lomond.

Breeding and growth
Flounders spawn in the open sea, the adults moving out of the rivers at the first frosts of winter. Each population has a definite spawning area, and some of these are known to fishermen, e.g. the flounders from the Irish Sea area spawn around the Morecambe Bay lightship. Flounder eggs float as soon as they are laid, and gradually drift inshore. A female may lay one million eggs. The period of spawning varies with the temperature, being between February and May. Flounders grow reasonably slowly, the young reaching 80–100 mm (3–4 in) by the end of the year in which they hatched, and 150 mm (6 in) by the next June (Wheeler 1979). Sexual maturity is reached when the male is only 12 cm (5 in) long, the female 18 cm (7 in). The maximum size is 51 cm (20 in) and a weight of about 3 kg (6½ lb).

The British rod-caught record is 2.59 kg (5 lb 11½ oz), caught by A. G. L. Cobbledick near Fowey, Cornwall in 1956.

Feeding
Flounders eat all types of animal food, but cockles and brown shrimps are especially favoured in the sea; various worms and *Gammarus* are probably more important in brackish water.

Fishing for flounders
Flounders are a popular angling species. A variety of baits are successful, but worms and shellfish, especially mussels and cockles, are probably the best; slipper limpets, soft-backed crabs, earthworms, prawns, fish and squid cuttings may also be successful.

The bait should be given some movement, either by pulling it slowly across the sand, or, in an estuary, letting it swim round in the current. Flounders take gently, so strikes should be slow and not made until the fish is felt to go off with the bait. Flounders can also be taken on spoons baited with a sliver of fish or piece of ragworm. These flounder spoons are made of white plastic and have the hook trailing some way (about 4 cm/1½ in) behind the spoon, and Trevor Horsby suggests that they look like a small fish dragging a juicy worm. The spoons should be dragged slowly across the bottom, disturbing little clouds of sand which the flounders find irresistible.

Flounders, and sometimes other flatfish, are caught by spearing in the shallow waters of an estuary. A barbed trident is the most efficient weapon, but in Donegal, where the sport is called 'forking for flushes' an ordinary hayfork with two curved prongs is used. Once the fish are speared they must be lifted smoothly and quickly into the boat. In some areas flounders are fished commercially with trammel nets which have arms of large mesh to guide the fish into the central finer mesh section. Flounders are generally considered inferior eating to other flatfish, the flesh having little taste.

Characteristics
Dorsal fin: about 60 rays.
Anal fin: 35–46 rays.

Flounder from Thames estuary. Photographed 26 October.

Sole from Thames estuary. Photographed 26 October.

Plaice, Sole, Dab and Brill

Plaice. *Pleuronectes platessa* Linn. Family *Pleuronectidae*; Sole. *Solea solea* Linn. Family *Soleidae*; Dab. *Limanda limanda* Linn. Family *Pleuronectidae*; Brill. *Scophthalmus rhombus* Linn. Family *Scopthalmidae*.

Recognition and related species
These four species of flatfish are primarily marine but small specimens are sometimes caught in estuaries and harbours.

The sole is rather elongated with a small mouth to one side of the rounded snout, and narrow parallel-sided fins along both sides of the body. The tail has a short and thick 'wrist'. The eyes are on the right-hand side of the head.

The dab is a wider fish than the sole, mainly because of its fins which are widest at the middle. Its snout is more pointed with the mouth at its apex. Its scales are finely toothed, which gives the skin a rough feel.

The plaice is similar to the dab in shape but has four to six bony knobs on its head, and smooth-edged rather than rough scales.

The brill is the most rounded of the flatfish likely to be encountered in estuaries. It differs from the others in having the eyes on the left-hand side of the head; it also has the first few rays of the dorsal fin free of membrane. The large rounded tail has a wide 'wrist'.

Habitat and distribution
The larger specimens of most of the flatfish live in the open sea, but the young (as shown here) begin their life inshore, in intertidal pools and in estuaries, usually on sandy or muddy bottoms.

The sole is found all round the coast of the British Isles, and from southern Norway southwards to west Africa and the western and northern coasts of the Mediterranean.

The dab is a more northern fish, also common round the British Isles, but found all round Norway and Iceland, and extending only as far south as the Bay of Biscay.

The plaice is even more widespread being found also around southern Greenland and in most of the Mediterranean except the far east.

The brill is a more southern species being rare north of England and Denmark, but common around the Mediterranean and the Black Sea.

Breeding and growth
All flatfish spawn in the open sea in spring and early summer, and the young fish swim near the surface before they metamorphose into the familiar adult shape and begin life on the bottom in shallow water. By this time they have drifted inshore. Most flatfish are long-lived and slow-growing, though large specimens are rare nowadays because of heavy fishing. The sole reaches a maximum weight of 3 kg (6 lb 10 oz), the dab 1.3 kg (2 lb 14 oz), the plaice 7 kg (15 lb 6 oz) and the brill 7.2 kg (16 lb). These are all small species compared with the halibut, a deepwater flatfish found in the subarctic waters of the North Atlantic. Specimens of 320 kg (706 lb) at 2.54 m (7 ft) long have been caught, and even larger ones up to 4 m (12 ft) long were reported in the past when they were less fished for, and more likely to live long enough to reach that size.

Feeding
Most bottom-living flatfish feed on small crustaceans, worms and molluscs, and sometimes small fish.

Fishing for flatfish
Casting from a sandy beach is the usual way to catch flatfish with rod and line. Plaice and the other species move into shallower water in mid-summer after spawning. Baits can vary from ragworms and various shellfish to pieces of squid and fish strips. It is often an advantage to give some movement to the bait, and a spoon, baited with a strip of fish or a worm, will often be successful.

All flatfish are excellent to eat, but some have a better reputation among gourmets. In general the brill is considered the best of the four species shown here, followed by the sole, the plaice and the dab.

Characteristics
Plaice: anal fin: 48–59. *Sole:* anal fin: 65–75
Dab: anal fin: 50–64. *Brill:* anal fin: 56–62, left-eyed.

Dab from Thames estuary. Photographed 26 October.

Brill from Thames estuary. Photographed 26 October.

Common gobies from Thames estuary. Photographed 26 October.

Common goby

Common goby. *Pomatoschistus microps* Kroyer. Family *Gobiidae*. French, gobie.

Recognition and related species

The common goby is one of the commonest estuarine fish, but is also found all along the shores in shallow water. It is rather like a small pale bullhead (although the two are not closely related), but its two dorsal fins are separate and the second dorsal fin and anal fin have much fewer rays. Both sexes have a dark spot on the base of the tail, and the males, especially at breeding time, have a spot on the first dorsal fin, and a dark throat.

There are seventeen other species of goby in northern Europe, but none regularly enter fresh or even brackish water. The commonest and most similar is the sand goby, *P. minutus*, which differs in having 58–70 rather than 39–52 scales along the lateral line, and a narrower 'wrist' to the tail than the common goby.

Habitat and distribution

The common goby is found all around the British Isles, and from the Baltic south to the western Mediterranean. It lives in shallow areas in the sea, in intertidal pools and especially on muddy or sandy shores and in estuaries. It extends into canals and rivers where the water is slightly brackish.

Breeding and growth

Spawning takes place in summer, from April to August, the eggs being laid on the hollow underside of a shell such as a cockle, and guarded by the male. Maximum length reached is 7 cm (2¾ in); 4–5 cm (1¼–2 in) is the usual adult range. Most specimens probably live less than two years.

Feeding

Gobies feed mainly on the larvae of crustaceans.

Fishing for gobies

Gobies have no known uses, though they are doubtless valuable as food for larger fish such as flounders and bass. Terns have been reported feeding on them. They would be a suitable quarry for children with nets in pools along the shore, and are also recommended as bait fish for pollack, coalfish or wrasse.

Characteristics

1st dorsal fin: 6 spines. 2nd dorsal fin: 10 rays.
Anal fin: 1 spine and 8 rays. Scales along the lateral line: 39–52.

Pouting

Pouting, pout, whiting pout, or bib. *Trisopterus luscus* Linn. Family *Gadidae*. French, tacaud.

Recognition and related species

The pouting or bib is a poor relation of the cod and haddock. Young fish are common in estuaries although it is essentially a marine species. It may be distinguished from other members of the cod family by its rather deep body, its three dorsal and two anal fins, all of which overlap, and by its pelvic fins, which overlap the first anal fin. The coppery sheen on the sides is also characteristic.

Habitat and distribution

Larger pouting are found in deeper water down to 300 m (1000 ft), the smaller inshore, particularly around submerged rocks and sunken wrecks. Young fish are common in large estuaries such as those of the Thames and Severn.

The pouting is found all round the British Isles, but is commonest in the south and west and from southern Norway to Morocco and the north-west Mediterranean.

Breeding and growth

Pouting spawn in moderately deep water from January to April. The eggs and larvae drift inshore, and young fish move into the estuaries in late autumn. By the end of their first summer they are 11–13 cm (4½–5 in), and 22–25 cm (8½–10 in) by the end of their third year. Maximum length is about 40 cm (16 in), and weight 2.5 kg (5 lb). The British rod-caught record is 2.49 kg (5 lb 8 oz), caught by R. S. Armstrong in 1969 off Berry Head.

Feeding

Mainly crustaceans, small squid and fish.

Angling for pouting

Pouting can be taken on small hooks and almost any of the baits used for seafish. They favour rocky ground, piers or any obstruction covered with weed. They are easy to catch, and popular for use as bait for cod, bass, congers, etc. The pouting has a poor reputation as a food fish because the flesh spoils very quickly (they are sometimes called 'stink alive'), but it is similar to whiting, and can be good enough if eaten fresh.

Characteristics

Dorsal fins: 3, all overlapping. Anal fins: 2.
Ventral fin: overlapping anal. Barbel: 1 well developed.

Grey mullet

Grey mullet. Family *Mugilidae*. French, muge; German, Meerasche; Dutch, harder; Italian, cephalo.

Recognition and related species

Grey mullets are very distinctive fish with torpedo-shaped bodies covered with large scales. They have two small and well-separated dorsal fins, the front (first) with four spiny rays, the rear (second) with mainly soft rays.

Three species are found in northern European waters:

thin-lipped grey mullet, *Mugil ramada* Risso;
thick-lipped grey mullet, *Mugil labrosus* Risso;
golden grey mullet, *Mugil auratus* Risso.

Three other species are found in the Mediterranean and on the Atlantic coast of Spain, Portugal and South France:

common grey mullet, *Mugil labeo* Cuvier;
striped grey mullet, *Mugil cephalus* Linn;
sharpnose grey mullet, *Mugil saliens* Risso.

The differences between the species are in the formation of the lips, the scaling on the head and the relative lengths of the head and the pectoral fins. For illustrations of all six species and for an identification key, readers can consult P. Maitland's *Guide to the Freshwater Fishes of Britain and Europe*.
The common British species can be distinguished as follows: in the thick-lipped grey mullet the pectoral fin, if folded forward, reaches the front edge of the eye, and there are no scales on the lower jaw; in the thin-lipped grey mullet the pectoral fin, if folded forward, does not reach the eye and the scales on the top of the head extend as far as or beyond the nostrils; in the golden grey mullet the body colour is golden rather than grey, and there is a distinct golden spot on the gill cover, the scales on the top of the head do not extend as far as the nostrils, and the pectoral fin, if folded forward, reaches the rearward edge of the eye. The more southern species are distinguished by similar characters: sharpnose grey mullet have several golden spots on the gill cover; common grey mullet have a very thick upper lip, as thick as the diameter of the eye; striped mullet have a fleshy eyelid covering much of the eye.

Habitat and distribution

Shoals of grey mullet are common in estuaries, harbours and coastal waters in summer and autumn. The thin-lipped grey mullet is the species most often found in fresh water and shoals can often be seen breaking the surface at the very head of tidal water. The other two British species are commoner in the sea and less often enter brackish water.
In the Mediterranean, grey mullet are important commercially and are caught in traps when they move into coastal rivers, lagoons and lakes. All the species mentioned here are found all around the Mediterranean, and (except *M. labeo*) in the Black Sea. The three northern species extend as far north as Scotland and Ireland, but the golden is the least common in these northern areas. Only the thick-lipped extends into the Baltic.

Breeding and growth

Grey mullet spawn in the sea in summer, usually near the coast.
The eggs are released into the sea and the fry probably grow rather slowly, reaching about 7.5 cm (3 in) in their first year. They mature very late, when three to five years old. Of the three northern species, the thick-lipped is the largest reaching about 75 cm (30 in) and a weight of 4.5 kg (10 lb), but anything over 2.5 kg (5 lb) is a very good specimen. The British rod-caught record for the thin-lipped grey mullet is 2.83 kg (6 lb 4 oz), caught by H. E. Mepham in the river Rother in Kent in 1981. The British rod-caught record for the thick-lipped grey mullet is 6.43 kg (14 lb 2 oz), caught by R. S. Gifford at Aberthaw, S. Wales in 1979. The British rod-caught record for the golden grey mullet is 1.20 kg (2 lb 10 oz), caught by F. Odoire at Platte Saline, Alderney in 1983.

Feeding

Mud is the staple diet of grey mullet. They feed by taking in mouthfuls of soft surface mud and filtering out algae and other edible matter, such as worms, small molluscs and crustaceans. To cope with this mainly algal diet, the mullet has a thick-walled gizzard-like stomach and a very long folded intestine, 2 m (7 ft) in a fish 27 cm (13 in) long.
Mullet soon learned that richer feeding was to be had in areas frequented by man. They often feed near the outlets of food factories such as creameries or abbatoirs, and become used to eating bread or other scraps thrown into harbours.

Fishing for mullet

No form of sea angling requires such care and delicate tackle as mullet fishing. They are nervous fish and the shoals are easily frightened. Their mouths are small and they prefer soft food, which does not easily stay on the hook; sizes 12 or 14 are usually recommended with 1.25–1.5 kg (2½–3 lb) nylon cast. Mullet feed at different depths, so that some form of float tackle is needed to keep the bait at the required depth. Possible baits are bread (flake, crust and paste), cheese, minced meat, fish, banana, small worms, maggots, peas (garden peas half-cooked) and cooked macaroni or spaghetti. The last is especially good if boiled in sugar and water; and a small piece about 2.5 cm (1 in) long should be used.
The strike should be made as soon as the float begins to move. Because mullet have soft mouths, a light rod should be used and they should be played carefully if the hook is not to tear free. Other methods have exciting possibilities. Trevor Housby goes into mullet fishing in more detail, and also recommends fishing floating bread crust as is used for carp, and spinning with a small spoon of the Mepps type, the hook trailing about 3.5 cm (1½ in) behind, baited with a small ragworm.

Cooking mullet

In England, mullet have never been highly regarded as food, but in the Mediterranean they are much sought after and appreciated, as they were in Roman times.
The flesh is firm and slightly oily, rather lighter than mackerel. It is excellent either grilled or baked in foil with herbs, oil and wine or lemon. Mullet roe is a valuable commodity, the basis of the true taramasalata, now often made with cod-roe, and botargo, dried and salted, and eaten in thin strips as an appetizer. Jane Grigson describes how it was formerly imported into England, and how Pepys records in his diary in June 1661 eating it on bread and butter, with great draughts of claret, in the company of Sir William Penn, father of Pennsylvania Penn.

Characteristics

1st dorsal fin: 4 spines. 2nd dorsal fin: 7 rays.
Anal fin: 8–9 rays. Scales along the lateral line: *c.* 45.

Littlehampton harbour, Sussex.

Thin-lipped grey mullet from Littlehampton. Photographed 26 July.

Estuary of river Arun, Sussex.

Bass

Bass, sea bass. *Dicentrarchus labrax* Linn. Family *Serranidae*.

Recognition and related species
This fine looking silvery coastal fish can be recognized by its two dorsal fins and rather slender body. Its head is large and rather rounded. It is most likely to be confused with a zander (p.76), but lacks the dark bars on its side, and its elongated head. It also has fewer spiny rays in its first dorsal fin (eight to nine) than either the zander or perch (p.74). The American largemouth or black bass (p.114) is easily distinguished by having its two dorsal fins joined, the mullets by having four-spined first dorsal fins well separated from the non-spiny second dorsal.
Another species of sea bass is found along the coasts of France, Spain and the western Mediterranean and north Africa. This is the spotted bass (*Dicentrarchus punctatus*), which differs mainly in its spotted sides, and in the comb-line margins of the scales between its eyes. *D. labrax* may have spots on its body when young, but these are not visible in the adults.

Habitat and distribution
The bass is found all round the coasts of the British Isles, and in the North Sea as far as southern Norway. It is also found on the Atlantic coast of Europe as far south as the Canary Islands, and throughout the Mediterranean and the Black Sea. It tends to be somewhat migratory, moving northwards into the southern North Sea in early summer (the first specimens are often seen in Kent in May) and moving south again in autumn. There are relatively few records from Scotland.
It inhabits estuaries and rocky and sandy coasts, often penetrating up into brackish water, especially when young. Bass may sometimes be seen inland of the breakers on a sandy beach or along the edges of an estuary, chasing sand-eels, their silver sides flashing underwater.

Breeding and growth
Bass spawn in the sea between March and June, attaching their eggs to rocks.
Growth is relatively slow, and a large specimen may be twenty years old. Fish of 3–3.5 kg (7–8 lb) are good specimens, the British rod-caught record being 8.33 kg (18 lb 6 oz), caught by R. G. Slater off Eddystone in 1975.

Feeding
Bass are predatory fish, and will eat almost any live animal. Shore crabs and prawns are commonly eaten, as are sand-eels, elvers and other small fish. Larger specimens, above about 3 kg (6 lb) are said to become scavengers and eat anything edible.

Fishing for bass
Bass can be caught on most kinds of bait, live or dead, on spoons or plugs or even large flies. Night fishing is often good and dawn a good taking time. Favoured baits are live prawns or sand-eels, razor fish, soft-shelled crabs or larger live bait such as small pouting. These should be fished in mid-water, especially around rocky headlands or reefs of rocks extending into a sandy bay. Spinning for bass is a popular and often successful method, and long wobbling spoons or pike spoons are recommended by Trevor Housby in his excellent book *Shore Fishing*. He also recommends plugs and wagtails, especially blue ones, all in large sizes.
Bottom fishing with a float or a leger can also be successful, especially where rocks jut out over a smooth bottom. Kipper fillets are excellent for this method, as are other fish and small squid or squid heads. Large baits can be used, as bass have large mouths, and big specimens in particular are attracted to large size baits. Surf casting on a strand is one of the most exciting ways of catching bass. The usual tackle to use is a paternoster, the bait sand-eels, fish strips or lugworms. Bass swim among the breakers (supposedly behind the third breaker) or even behind them in a few feet of water, looking for food that has been disturbed by the waves.

Cooking bass
Bass are excellent to eat; their flesh is white and rather soft, and for this reason Jane Grigson (*Fish Cookery*, 1973) recommends that they should be baked, or fried, as steaks, in butter.
Everything possible should be done to conserve stocks of bass. Small specimens should be carefully returned to the water alive. Because they are at the northern end of their range in the British Isles and so probably do not breed successfully every season, and because they grow relatively slowly, bass are very susceptible to over-fishing and only large specimens which are needed for eating should be killed.

Characteristics
1st dorsal fin: 8–9 spines.
2nd dorsal fin: 2–3 spines, 9–11 rays.
Anal fin: 2 spines, 9–10 rays.
Scales along the lateral line: more than 70.

Selected Bibliography

Banarescu, P., Blanc, M., Gaudet, J.-L., Hureau, J.-C., *European Inland Water Fish – Multilingual Catalogue*, FAO/FNB 1971.

Cacutt, L., *British Freshwater Fish – the Story of their Evolution*, Croom Helm 1979.

Campbell, R. N., 'Ferox Trout, *Salmo trutta* and *Salvelinus alpinus* in Scottish Lochs', *J. Fish Biol.* 14:1–29 (1979).

Coles, T. F., *Anglian Water Authority Fisheries Reports*, 1978–80.

Fahy, E. and Warren W. P., 'Long-lived Sea Trout, Sea Run "Ferox"?' *Salmon and Trout Mag.* 227:72–5 (1984).

Ferguson, A. and Mason F. M., 'Alloenzyme Evidence for Reproductively Isolated Sympatric Populations of Brown Trout, *Salmo trutta* L. in Lough Melvin', *J. Fish Biol.* 18:629–642 (1981).

Ferguson, A., Himberg, K.-J., and Svardson, G., 'Systematics of the Irish Pollan', *J. Fish Biol.* 12:221–233 (1978).

Housby, T., *Shore Fishing*, Pan 1974.

Jenkins, J. Travis, *The Fishes of the British Isles*, Warne 1925.

Jones, J. W., *The Salmon*, Collins 1959.

Maitland, P. S., *Freshwater Fishes of Britain and Europe*, Hamlyn 1977.

— — 'A Key to the Freshwater Fishes of the British Isles', *Sci. Publ. Freshw. Biol. Ass.* 27:1–39 (1972).

— — 'Origin and Present Distribution of *Coregonus* in the British Isles', Lindsay and Woods (eds.), *Biology of Coregonid Fishes*, pp.99–114 (1970).

Mason, B. J., *The Current Status of Research on Acidification of Surface Waters*, Royal Society 1984.

Maxwell, H., *British Freshwater Fishes*, Hutchinson 1904.

Newdyke, J., *The Complete Freshwater Fishes of the British Isles*, A. and C. Black 1979.

Orton, D. A. (ed.), *Where to Fish 1982–83*, A. and C. Black 1982.

Regan, C. Tate, *British Freshwater Fishes*, Methuen 1911.

Slack, H. D., Gervers, F. W. K. and Hamilton, J. D., *The Biology of the Powan in Studies in Loch Lomond*, I:113–127 (1957), Glasgow Univ. Publ.

Sosin, M. and Clark, J., *Through the Fish's Eye*, Andre Deutsch, 1976.

Spillman, C. J., *Poisson d'Eau Douce*, Le Chevalier, Paris 1961.

Svardson, G., 'Speciation in Scandinavian *Coregonus*', *Rep. Inst. FF.*, Drottningholm 55:144–171 (1979).

Vostradovsky, J., *Freshwater Fishes*, Hamlyn 1973.

Walker, C. F., (ed.) *The Complete Flyfisher*, Barrie and Jenkins 1976.

Walker, R., *Stillwater Angling*, Pan 1975.

Wheeler, Alwyne, *Key to the Fishes of Northern Europe*, Warne 1978.

— — *The Tidal Thames*, Routledge and Kegan Paul 1979.

Wootton, R. J., *A Functional Biology of the Sticklebacks*, Croom Helm 1984.

Index

Aal 122
able de Heckel 79
ablette 78
Abramis ballerus 92
 brama 88
 sapa 92
Acipenser stellatus 125
 sturio 125
Aland 84
Alburnoides bipunctatus 57
Alburnus alburnus 78
allis shad 126
Alosa alosa 126
 fallax 126
alose feinte 126
alver 78
Ambloplites rupestris 112
American brown bullhead 110
 catfish 110
 brook trout 24
anadelo 54
Anguilla anguilla 122
 rostrata 122
ankerias 122
apron 54
Arctic charr 15
Aristotle's catfish 108
Asche 44
asp 80
Aspertrigla cuculus 129
Aspius aspius 80
 vorax 80

Baars 74
Bachneunauge 52
Bachforelle 26
Bachsaibling 24
bäcknejonöga 52
backoring 26
bar 140
barbe 64
barbeau fluviatile 64
 meridionale 62
 truite 62
barbeel 64
barbel 64
barbel, Mediterranean 62
barbo canino 62
Barbus barbus 64
 comiza 64
 meridionalis 62
 prespensis 62
Barsch 74
barse 74
bass 140
 black 114
 largemouth 114
 rock 112
 sea 140
 smallmouth 114
beekforel 26
beek prik 52
beekridder 15
belica 79
beluga 125
bergsimpa 50
bib 136
bitterling 110
bittervoorn 110
bjorkna 90
black bass 114
black bullhead 110
blageon 56
blasik 43
Blaufelchen 43
blankvoorn 82
bleak 78
Blicca bjoerkna 90
blue bream 92
blue gurnard 128

bondelle 41
bordelière 90
bot 132
bouviere 110
Brachsen 88
brasen 88
braxen 88
bream, bronze 88
 blue 92
 common 88
 Danubian 92
 silver 90
 white 90
 whiteye 92
breamflat 90
breme 88
brême 90
brill 134
bronforel 24
bronze bream 88
brook lamprey 52
brook trout 24
brown trout 26
brochet 70
bullhead 50
 American brown 110
 black 110
 Siberian 50
burbot 118

Capelin 130
carassin 102
Carassius auratus 100
 carassius 102
carp, common 96
 crucian 102
 gibel 100
 grass 104
 king 101
 leather 99
 mirror 99
 Prussian 100
 wild 97
carpe 96
catfish 108
 American 110
 Aristotle's 108
 Channel 110
cephalo 138
chabot 50
Channel catfish 110
charr 15
 Arctic 15
 speckled 24
chekhon 124
chevin 68
chevaine 68
Chondrostoma colchicum 66
 genei 66
 kneri 66
 nasus 66
 oxyrhynchum 66
 phoxinus 66
 polylepis 66
 soetta 66
 toxostoma 58
chub 68
chum salmon 18
Cobitis taenia 120
common bream 88
common carp 96
Coregonus acronius 40
 albula 42
 autumnalis 43
 autumnalis pollan 40, 43
 clupeoides 43
 fera 40
 lavaretus 40, 41
 nilssoni 40
 oxyrhinchus 41
 pallasi 40
 tryboni 42
 vandesius 42
 wartmanni 7, 40, 43

Cottus gobio 50
 poecilopus 50
crucian carp 102
Ctenopharyngodon idella 104
cull 50
cut-throat trout 36
cuzean 46
Cyprinus carpio 96

Dab 134
dace 60
 Croatian 56
Danubian bream 92
Danubian salmon 18
dauphin 54
Dicentrarchus labrax 140
 punctatus 140
Döbel 68
dolly varden 15
durgan 62
dwergmeerval 110

Eel 122
eel pout 118
Egli 74
elft 126
Elritze 46
eperlan 130
epinoch 116
epinochette 117
Esox lucius 70
 masquinongy 70
 reichteri 70
esturgeon 125

Faren 92
färna 68
Felchen 40
'ferox' trout 28
fifteen-spined stickleback 117
finnock 32
fint 126
Finte 126
flet 132
flodrejonoga 52
Flounder 132
fluke 132
Flussneunauge 52
Forellenbarsch 114
French nase 58

Gädda 70
gangfish 41
gardon 82
gars 78
Gasterosteus aculeatus 116
gestippelde alver 57
gibel carp 100
gillaroo trout 28
glane 108
gobie 136
Gobio gobio 94
goby, common 136
 sand 136
golden orfe 85
 tench 106
 trout 36
Goldfisch 100
goldfish 100
gös 76
goudvis 100
goujon 94
Graeskarpe 104
grande alose 126
grass carp 104
grayling 44
green sunfish 112
grey gurnard 128
grey mullet 138
gremille 78
grilse 20
grönling 48
groplöja 79
Groppe 50
Gründling 94

gudgeon 94
gulfisk 100
gurnard 128
 blue 128
 grey 128
 red 128
 tub 128
 yellow 128
Güster 90
gwyniad 40
Gymnocephalus acerina 78
 cernuus 78
 schraetser 78

harjus 44
harr 44
Hasel 60
hauki 70
Hecht 70
horned pout 110
hotu 66
houting 41
Hucho hucho 18
 taimen 18
humpback salmon 18
Huso huso 125
harder 138

Ictalurus melas 110
 nebulosus 110
 punctatus 110
id 84
ide 84
insjooring 26

Jack 70
jarvitaimen 26
jarvisiika 41

Kamloops 36
Kaulbarsh 78
Karausche 102
karp 96
Karpe 96
karper 96
king carp 101
kirjoevasimppu 50
kirjoloki 36
kleine Marane 42
kleine Modderkruiper 120
kleine Schebranke 40
kolblei 90
krohle 130
kuka 76
küski 78
kvid 46
kwabaal 118
kynnenpiikki 117

Lachs 18
lahna 88
lake trout 24
lampern 52
Lampetra fluviatilis 52
 planeri 52
lampoire de rivière 52
lamprey, brook 52
 river 52
 sea 52
largemouth bass 114
lax 18
leather carp 99
Lepomis auritus 112
 cyanellus 112
 gibbosus 112
Leucaspius delineatus 79
 irideus 79
 marathonicus 79
 stymphalicus 79
Leuciscus cephalus 68
 idus 84
 leuciscus 60
 polylepis 56
 souffia 56
Limanda limanda 134

loach, spined 120
   stone 49
   weather 120
loche de rivière 120
loche franche 48
loggerhead 68
lohi 18
loja 78
Lota lota 118
lote de rivière 118
loup 140

Made 118
madrilla 58
Maifisch 126
maisild 126
mal 108
Mediterranean barbel 62
melanote 84
Meerasche 138
Meerforelle 32
meerval 108
meun 68
Micropterus dolomieui 114
  salmoides 114
miekkasärki 124
miller's thumb 50
minnow 46
   poznan 46
   swamp 46
Misgurnus fossilis 120
mirror carp 99
miukku 42
Moderlieschen 79
monni 108
mort 82
muge 138
Mugil auratus 138
  cephalaus 138
  labeo 138
  labrosus 138
  ramada 138
  saliens 138
mullet, grey 138
musard 66
muskellunge 70
mutu 46

Nase 66
Näsling 66
Nerophis ophidion 128
nieria 15
nissoga 120
Noemacheilus barbatulus 48

Oal 118
omble-chevalier 15
ombre commun 44
Oncorhynchus gorbuscha 18
  keta 18
orfe 84
öring 32
Osmerus eperlanus 130

Paling 122
parr, rainbow trout 38
  salmon 18
  sea trout 32
Pelecus cultratus 124
Perca fluviatilis 74
perch 74
perche 74
perche-soleil 112
persico sole 112
petite lampoire 52
Petromyzon marinus 52
petite marène 42
Phoxinus czekanowskii 46
  percnurus 46
  phoxinus 46
piikkimonni 110
pike 70
pike-perch 76
pipefish 128
plaice 134
planktonsik 40

Platichthys flesus 139
Pleuronectes platessa 134
Plötze 82
poisson chat 110
poisson rouge 100
Pomatoschistus microps 136
  minutus 136
pope 78
pos 78
pout 136
pout, eel 118
  horned 110
  whiting 136
pouting 136
powan 7, 40, 43
Prussian carp 100
pumpkinseed 112
Pugnitius platygaster 117
  pugnitius 117
puro taimen 26
puronieria 24

Quappe 118

rainbow trout 36
rapjen 80
red gurnard 129
redbrest sunfish 112
Regenbogenforelle 36
regenboogforel 36
regenbage 36
Rhodeus sericeus 110
Rhone Streber 54
river-spawning whitefish 41
rivierdonderpad 50
riviergrondel 94
rivierprik 52
roach 82
rock bass 112
roding 15
roi poisson 54
rotengle 86
Rotfeder 86
ruda 102
rudd 86
ruffe 78
Rutilus rutilus 82
Russnase 124

salakka 78
Salmo aquabonita 36
  clarkei 36
  gairdneri 36
  nigripinnis 28
  salar 18
  stomachius 28
  trutta 26
  trutta caspius 32
  trutta fario 26
  trutta labrax 32
  trutta macrostigma 26
  trutta trutta 32
Salmothymus ochridanus 18
  obtusirostris 18
salmon 18
  chum 18
  Danubian 18
  humpback 18
  parr 18
Salvelinus alpinus 15
  fontinalis 24
  fimbriatus 15
  gracillimus 15
  malma 15
  namaycash 24
  perisii 15
  scharfii 15
  struanensis 15
  willughbii 15
sampi 125
sandkrypare 94
sandre 76
särki 82

sarv 86
saumon 18
saumon de fontaine 24
sayne 84
Scardinius erythrophthalmus 86
schelly 40
Schleie 106
Schmerle 48
Schnapel 41
Schneider 57
Scophthalmus rhombus 134
sea bass 140
  lamprey 52
  trout 32
seebeasch 140
Seeforelle 26
See-saibling 15
serpeling 60
sevrjuga 125
sewin 32
Siberian bullhead 50
Sibirische Groppe 50
siika 41
sikloja 42
sik 41
silure 108
Silurus aristotelis 108
  glanis 108
  triostegus 108
silver bream 90
sinetz 92
skelly 68
skrubbskädda 132
smallmouth bass 114
smaspigg 117
smelt 131
smolt 18, 32
sneep 66
snoek 70
snoekaars 76
Soiffe 58
Solea solea 134
Sole 134
Sonnenbarsch 112
sorcier 54
soufie 56
speckled charr 24
  trout 24
spiering 130
Spinachia spinachia 117
spined loach 120
spirlin 57
spotted bass 140
staksill 126
stäm 60
stärkniv 124
steelhead 36
Steinbeisser 120
stekelbaars 116
stensimpa 50
steur 125
Stichling 116
stickleback, fifteen-spined 117
  ten-spined 117
  three-spined 116
  Ukranian 117
Stint 130
Stizostedion lucioperca 76
  volgensis 76
stone loach 49
stör 125
storspigg 116
Streber 54
  Rhone 54
Stromer 56
sturgeon 125
suiffe 56
sulkava 92
sunfish, green 112
  redbrest 112
sutane 106
syngnathe 128

Syngnathus abaster 128
  acus 128
  rostellatus 128
  typhle 128

Tacaud 136
taimen 18
taimen (Finnish) 32
tanche 106
ten-spined stickleback 117
tench 106
  golden 106
  vermilion 106
three-spined stickleback 116
Thymallus thymallus 44
tiendoornige stekelbaars 117
Tinca tinca 106
Trigla lucerna 128
trigle 128
Trisopterus luscus 136
trout 26
  American brook 24
  brown 26
  cut-throat 36
  'ferox' 28, 31, 32
  golden 36
  gillaroo 28
  rainbow 36
  sea 32
  slob 26
  speckled 24
Truite arc-en-ciel 36
  de lac 26
  de mer 32
  de rivière 26
toutain 80
toxostome 58
tub gurnard 128
tubfish 128
twaite shad 126

Ukelei 78
Ukranian stickleback 117

Vandoise 60
vairon 46
vairone 56
vendace 40, 42
vermilion tench 106
vetje 79
vimba 124
Vimba vimba 124
vima 124
vimpa 124

Waller 108
Wandersaibling 15
weather loach 120
Wels 108
wild carp 97
winde 84
white bream 90
white trout 32
whitefish 40, 43
whitefish, river-spawning 41
whiteye bream 92
whitling 32

yellow gurnard 128

Zahrte 124
Zander 76
zeebaars 140
zeeforel 32
zeelt 106
Ziege 124
Zingel asper 54
  streber 54
  zingel 54
zonnebaars 112
Zope 92
zwartebaars 114
Zwergstickling 117
Zwergurels 110

The Library
Writtle Agricultural College
Nr. Chelmsford Essex